The Path
to Partnership

A Guide for Junior Associates

Steven C. Bennett

Westport, Connecticut
London

Library of Congress Cataloging-in-Publication Data

Bennett, Steven C., 1957–
    The path to partnership : a guide for junior associates / Steven C. Bennett
      p. cm
Includes bibliographic references and index.
    ISBN 0-275-98106-1 (alk. paper)
  1. Law—Vocational guidance—United States. 2. Law partnership—United
States. I. Title.
    KF300.B36 2004
    340′.023′73—dc22   2003063701

British Library Cataloguing in Publication Data is available.

Library of Congress Catalog Card Number: 2003063701
ISBN: 0-275-98106-1

First published in 2004

Praeger Publishers, 88 Post Road West, Westport, CT 06881
An imprint of Greenwood Publishing Group, Inc.
www.praeger.com

Printed in the United States of America

The paper used in this book complies with the
Permanent Paper Standard issued by the National
Information Standards Organization (Z39.48-1984).

10 9 8 7 6 5 4 3 2 1

Copyright Acknowledgments

In loving memory of my parents,
Rollie G. Bennett and Norma A. Nelson Bennett.

Contents

Acknowledgments

I wish to acknowledge, gratefully, the support and encouragement provided by my law firm for teaching and writing endeavors. The views expressed in this book, however, are solely my own and should not be attributed to the law firm or its clients. I also wish to acknowledge the many students and junior lawyers with whom I have had the privilege to work. Their experiences and insights are a vital part of this book. Finally, I wish to acknowledge my family (Suzanne, Danielle, and Nicole) for giving me the time and the inspiration to write this book.

Acknowledgments

Introduction

I have been a lawyer for more than 18 years. In that time, I have gone through many of the hard knocks and challenges that the legal profession presents. Much of the learning that comes from such experiences cannot be taught in a book or by lecture. The process of professional maturation is individual, and each lawyer finds his or her own way.

Still, in those 18 years, I have worked extensively with junior lawyers and law students as a teacher at Fordham University School of Law and the Brooklyn Law School, also as a supervisor at the Office of the United States Attorney for the Southern District of New York. Most recently, for more than 5 years, I served as co-coordinator for the New Associates Group in the New York City offices of Jones Day.

What I have learned from those experiences is that junior lawyers can often have a tough time entering the practice of law. Law school, unfortunately, provides mostly "book learning" about the law: how to conduct legal research and think like a lawyer. It teaches very little about the practical aspects of lawyering or the daily life of a lawyer in a law firm.

What I have also learned is that many of the problems that junior lawyers face can be predicted. Over the years, I have seen the same kinds of problems arise again and again. The individual circumstances may vary, but the problems remain relatively similar.

The principal focus of this book is the junior lawyer just starting out in the practice of law at a law firm. The aim of the book is to expose some of the common problems and challenges that junior lawyers face, and to offer some practical solutions for some of those problems. My great hope is that junior lawyers who read this book will recognize that they are not alone, that others have struggled, and survived, through the process of becoming a lawyer.

This book is not a panacea. It represents the opinions of one lawyer, with one set of experiences. This book does not address every problem and does not suggest every possible solution. This book is, at best, a starting point for the journeys that junior lawyers take.

Getting Started

IS LAW FIRM LIFE FOR YOU?

Law school can create a kind of mass hysteria. The rush toward law firm recruiting (interviews with firms even in the first year, summer associate experiences, then a planned permanent associate position by the third year) can be so strong that law students may be caught up in the illusion that the only thing available (and the only thing desirable) after law school is work in a law firm. Because on-campus interviewing is typically dominated by major firms, moreover, the illusion extends to the assumption that the brass ring to grab must be work at some major firm after school.

But there is more (much more) to life in the law. The decision to pursue a career at a law firm should include consideration of these alternatives. In particular, it should involve a comparison of the advantages and disadvantages of law firm life versus these many other alternatives. The balancing of these considerations, of course, is purely an individual matter. This section thus is meant to identify some relevant issues for you to consider, rather than to suggest what may be right for you.

Expert versus Generalist

Are you already an expert in a particular business segment, technology, or area of the law? Do you hope to develop and exploit that expertise in a legal career? Or, are you starting from scratch, with no preconceptions of what might be right for you, or where you see yourself becoming an expert?

To a large extent, law firms (especially large law firms) in the early years of practice tolerate and even encourage the generalist instinct.

Aside from making a broad choice (corporate practice versus litigation, for example), it is often possible to spend the first few years of practice in a law firm gathering general experience, which could be applied in many different directions later in a career. Eventually, after some years of experience in a law firm, you may choose to focus quite heavily on a specific business segment or area of law. Many lawyers in law firms, however, remain generalists (within broad outlines) for a very long time (even an entire career).

By contrast, legal work in-house at a corporation, and in many areas of government, academia, and social service, usually requires a focus on a specific segment of the economy and/or on a specific area of the law. If, for example, you were to go to an in-house legal position at a publishing firm, you would need to develop expertise about the customs and practices of the publishing industry. You would also probably need to develop expertise in intellectual property matters (copyright, licensing, and the like), as well as (perhaps) develop some expertise in defamation and First Amendment issues. In addition, of course, you would need to learn the details of the operations of the publishing house (its history, corporate structure, key players, and major business issues) and any specifics relevant to your particular function. If you were, for example, charged with overseeing the publishing firm's electronic publishing activities from a legal perspective, you would need to know a great deal about electronic rights, the operation of the Internet, privacy, and other issues that have arisen with the new technologies of electronic publishing. In short, you would have to immerse yourself in the details of the business and become a true expert in matters related to that business (and perhaps even a subspecialty within the business).

Of course, it is also quite possible to become an expert (sometimes quite quickly) in a law firm. By working closely with a particular client or set of clients in an industry, you may gain much of the same broad grounding in the issues and practical aspects of law and business as an in-house lawyer in that industry might gain. "Boutique" law firms that specialize in particular industry or legal segments often claim this as one of their values. Even within larger law firms, industry practice teams often aim to create specialized expertise within the larger framework of general services that the law firm offers.

Which is right for you—generalist or expert? Generalists often have the luxury of trying out several different areas of business and the law to find what they most prefer. If any area of business or law becomes stale or moribund, moreover, generalists are often well-suited to find and develop new areas of interest.

Those who drive to become experts early on, by contrast, often have the ability to move ahead more quickly in terms of responsibility and real understanding, which can be quite satisfying as well. Experts, moreover, are often quite in demand. It may be easier for prospective employers to hire experts, when the employers know that they have specific slots to fill, rather than generalists (who fulfill no specific role).

Slow versus Fast

The rhythm of professional life in different positions can vary greatly. Generally, law firm assignments (especially in large law firms) are longer term, and tend to proceed more slowly, than assignments in a corporation. Typically, corporations and other major institutions hire law firms to perform work (handling major litigation, negotiating and documenting substantial deals, counseling on multifaceted and diffi-cult issues) that they do not have the resources to handle efficiently on their own. As a result, law firm lawyers tend to have more time to study the details of a problem and to assemble a comprehensive solution (often with a relatively large team of lawyers involved).

The rhythm may be even more relaxed in other settings, such as academia. Most law professors have the great luxury of time to study the details of their subject, to master its nuances, and to keep very current with developments in their preferrred area of the law.

In-house counsel at a corporation often have to move at a much faster pace in addressing problems, touching an issue only long enough to perform basic triage: Is this something that does not matter much? Is this something that matters, that I can handle myself? Is this something that matters, and on which I need help from others within the corpora-tion (or perhaps from an outside law firm)? A day in the life of an in-house lawyer can involve many such issues, quickly raised and quickly resolved. The result may be broad experience in addressing a variety of issues relevant to the in-house counsel's position, but less time to focus on any one single problem.

Government and social service agency work may go in either direc-tion. Work as in-house agency counsel is often similar to work in-house at a corporation (although the issues may be very different). Work as outside or litigation counsel (at the United States Attorney's office, State Attorney General's office, or city law department, for example) is often more like work at a law firm.

Pure Law versus Business

Legal work may be arrayed on a spectrum between pure law posi-tions and those that involve mostly business and practical issues.

Generally, the purest of the pure law positions is life in academia. There are those who find the concept of pure law work quite attractive. Instead of the burdens of searching for work, and handling administrative details in dealing with clients and managing the affairs of a business, there is often the freedom to focus on matters of personal interest in the law. An academic setting, in this sense, often provides the administrative structure and support that can permit such intellectual freedom.

Many positions, however, can combine elements of pure law with a more practical focus. Some academicians, for example, maintain some connections to the practice of law (supervising clinical programs at a law school, serving as "of counsel" to a law firm, or providing consulting services to a government or social service agency).

So, too, even within law firms and government or social service agencies, there may be opportunities to pursue some (perhaps even a great deal) of the pure law work that you might find attractive. Judicial clerkships, for example, often have substantial elements of pure law work (even though the practical business of processing cases is key). Many government agencies (such as the United States Solicitor General's office, and equivalent agencies that focus on appellate work before state and federal courts) are largely engaged in pure law work. So, too, many law firms have established niche appellate departments, aiming to focus a relatively small group of lawyers on the arcane and complicated issues that can often determine success in the appellate context. Social service agencies, moreover, often focus on important and developing legal issues affecting their constituencies. It may be possible to do substantial pure law work on such issues.

For most lawyers in most law firms, law firm life offers a combination of pure law, especially at the earliest stages (research and writing), with increasing focus on business and practical issues. To a degree, litigators (who often must research novel legal issues as part of their argumentation) hold on to more pure law experience longer.

Yet, inevitably, with seniority in a law firm, business and practical issues become ever more important. Business development and client contact are key aspects of success. Increasing responsibility for administrative aspects of the firm is also the norm.

This business and practical focus may be particularly pronounced at smaller firms. Indeed, if you begin your career as a solo practitioner, you will be plunged immediately into such issues.

Even in the government and social service settings, there is an element of business and practical concern that cannot be escaped. Agency administrators are very much clients to whom their counsel must report. And the practical aspects of running an institution (budgeting, expense control, and other administrative obligations) greatly affect the experiences of most government and social service lawyers.

In-house at a corporation, the focus often will be primarily on business and practical issues rather than pure law. Many in-house lawyers need do little legal research to solve most of their problems, relying largely on their general experience (and in-depth advice from their outside counsel, when necessary).

This is not to say that in-house counsel avoid participation in seminars, CLE programs, and bar committees, where they can keep up with important developments in their areas of interest; just the opposite. But those activities provide the backdrop for their more practical day-to-day experience.

Indeed, in-house counsel can often cross the line from lawyer to businessperson. In small ventures, in-house counsel may do double duty (as both lawyer and businessperson) to economize. Lawyers may also hold substantial personal financial stakes in such ventures. In larger institutions, counsel may transform their roles into more responsibility for business issues than legal issues simply for the enjoyment and satisfaction of conquering new challenges.

Almost always, however, in an in-house corporate position there is keen awareness of the imperatives of the business. Budgets and financial planning are critical. New business activities (mergers and divestitures, program initiatives, arrivals and departures of senior personnel) can have great effects on the experience of the in-house lawyer. Developments in pure areas of law, by comparison, generally hold much less immediate significance.

Credentials versus Preferences

There is a real temptation in law school to view the job search process as a giant, zero-sum competitive game. On that view, the aim of law school is to assemble the best set of credentials possible (best school, best grades, best law journal, etc.). Those best credentials, in turn, match up with a grid of potential career pursuits. That you are well-enough credentialed to get one of these "best" jobs, however, does not necessarily mean that you will be satisfied by such a job. Indeed, taking a job just because it appears to have high prestige cuts out the most important part of the search for a sustaining, rewarding legal career: self-assessment.

You must begin by looking at the aspects of various potential positions that are most important to you. Some potentially relevant factors were outlined earlier.

Some additional factors are quite obvious (salary, location, size of firm, area of concentration, etc.). Still others (such as the quality and social impact of the work) will be quite subjective and unique to you. Long term, if the factors that matter to you do not match with the characteristics of the job, you will not be satisfied, no matter how much other people tell you that you should be satisfied.

On the other hand, even if your credentials do not permit you to obtain your ideal position immediately, careful analysis of what truly matters to you will help you to find a position that comes closest to your ideal. Moreover, awareness of your true desires will make it easier for you to dedicate yourself to continuing to gain experience and to continuing to look for opportunities that may make it possible for you to move closer and closer to your ideal.

LAW SCHOOL PREPARATION FOR A LAW FIRM

Law school can be a very isolated world. The focus of most law schools (casebooks and lectures) may offer little insight into the practical work that goes on in law firms. Law students with no firsthand experience in a law firm, moreover, may have little direct knowledge of what will be expected of them upon their entry into a law firm. Indeed, it may be tempting for a law student essentially to ignore the practice of law that is to come. Although law students may spend a tremendous amount of time thinking about how to get a job and reviewing the characteristics of law firms to determine what seems to be the best job, they may spend much less time really preparing to do the job after graduation. Because, for many students, it does not seem possible to prepare for the full-time practice of law, some law students may simply drift through law school, marking time until graduation and entry into the real world of law.

But is there another way? Can law school actually help prepare you for life in a law firm? This section suggests some strategies that can help make law school more relevant to your future career in a law firm.

Begin with a candid self-assessment. Compare your skills and your experiences with the skills and experiences of a practicing lawyer. If you obtained a psychology undergraduate degree (as I did) and worked as a janitor during summers in college (as I did), you may have to go a long way to develop skills and experiences necessary for the practice of law. Law school can help. Viewed from the perspective of your future career in a law firm, you will need to take courses in the fundamentals of business (such as accounting for lawyers, commercial law, corporation law, and anything to do with finance). In your spare time (summers, for example) pick up a primer on the basics of business operations. If your law school permits it, consider taking an introductory business course at the undergraduate or graduate level.

Identify, in broad terms, your interests. Are you most likely headed for litigation? There are highly relevant law school courses: alternative dispute resolution, appellate practice, conflicts of law, evidence, federal courts, state civil procedure (New York practice), and trial advocacy. If you are more likely to become a business practice lawyer, consider: bankruptcy, mergers and acquisitions, securities regulation, and uniform commercial code. There are also some in-betweener courses that will likely help no matter which direction you go: administrative law and taxation, for example. Study of competition law (antitrust, copyright, patents, and trademarks) may similarly help you no matter what your eventual area of practice. There are, moreover, many specific courses that can be highly relevant to work in specific areas of law after graduation (criminal procedure, entertainment and sports law, family law, health law, immigration law, insurance law, labor and employment law, maritime law, product liability, trusts and estates, to name just a few).

Look for practical training in school. Many law schools now include clinical programs, internships, and other opportunities to learn practical skills. These programs can provide the best of both worlds, offering practical experience with the assistance of teachers who are focused on student education, rather than simply completing the practical tasks without meaningful feedback (as may happen at some law jobs).

Emphasize writing. It is not possible to overemphasize the importance of solid writing skills for success in a law firm. No matter what your ultimate pursuit, the ability to write well will benefit you throughout your career. Get journal (or moot court) experience if you can. If not, take at least one course with a paper requirement, where you can benefit from the experience of having your writing carefully critiqued, and learn the discipline of self-editing. If your school offers an upper-level advanced legal writing course, consider taking that course (or consider becoming a teaching assistant for the first-year legal writing course).

Recognize that law school is not an aptitude test. It is quite possible that a law school course (or professor) may awaken an interest in a subject for you and lead you to explore additional training, experience, and job placement that will expand upon that interest. The reverse, however, is not necessarily the case. A poorly taught course, or one in which you do not immediately excel, hardly means that you are prohibited from pursuing the same subject matter in your work after graduation. If you have a strong interest in a practice area, do not let a single negative law school experience prevent you from pursuing your goal.

Look for practical experience outside school. In addition to summer associate experiences, it may be possible to fit part-time legal work into your schedule during law school (especially during your final law school year). Your school may have relationships with specific firms for internship purposes, or you may find such part-time experience through your own inquiry. When interviewing for a summer associate position, for example, you may also want to inquire about a firm's part-time employment opportunities. Many schools, moreover, have connections to *pro bono* programs that can provide both practical experience and tremendous personal rewards. Look for experiences that may relate to your future endeavors, but be open to the possibility that even unrelated experiences can provide you with valuable insight into the fundamentals of legal practice: fact-gathering, legal research, legal analysis, drafting, negotiation, and oral communication. Strive, wherever possible, to supplement your book learning with some form of real-world experience.

Seek out faculty with practical experience. Many schools employ adjunct faculty who are engaged in the full-time practice of law, and many full-time law professors consult with law firms or maintain a smaller practice of law in addition to their academic endeavors. Often, merely talking to professors who have worked (or who are currently working) in your preferred area may give you valuable insights. Ask your professors what they like (and dislike) about their practice, what they thought was valuable (or not so valuable) preparation for that practice, and where they might advise a law student to consider working to gain the appropriate experience. Better yet, it may be possible to work directly with such professors (helping write an article or book chapter, or perhaps even working on a practical project).

Seek out alumni with practical experience. Many law schools have programs to place law students with alumni mentors. Take advantage of such a program, if your school offers it. Even if no formal program exists, consider reaching out to graduates (especially those with whom you are acquainted) to ask questions about their experiences and seek guidance on the best way to prepare for the practice of law. Your school's development and placement offices will likely have lists of graduates and some information on their current areas of practice. In addition, your school may host alumni receptions and education programs that attract alumni. Consider attending those programs and making connections with alumni, who are often eager to help students at their *alma mater* begin successful careers.

Limit pure academic study. Although individual courses may be interesting and insightful, an entire law school career of legal history, jurisprudence, or review of social problems is generally not good preparation for a law firm. Use your time wisely. Take such courses to broaden your horizons and stimulate your mind, not as a substitute for the "grind" practical courses that you know you should be taking.

Be a skeptical consumer. Law school, like most things, generally costs too much. Worse than paying too much, however, is the prospect of getting too little out of school. In choosing courses, and in deciding whether to stay in a course, apply a simple cost-benefit test: Is this course a waste of my time and money? If it is, find something better.

Prepare for the transition. The end of law school comes all too quickly. If you allow it to happen, you may find yourself near the end of school without a clear concept of what you really want to do with your career and where you should best start after law school. To avoid that syndrome, begin thinking early in law school where you might want your career to go. Spend lots of time at your school's placement center. Get to know the counselors, and make sure they get to know you. Identify alternative career paths and the kinds of skills required to follow each one. Eliminate clearly inappropriate alternatives. Place emphasis on finding what is stimulating and rewarding for you, rather than seeking to maintain generalist credentials forever.

Consider transition career steps. Judicial clerkships, government service and public service positions, for example, can provide practical experience between law school and practice in a law firm. Some postgraduate fellowships and study abroad, moreover, offer additional time to consider alternatives before leaping into full-time practice. Some students, moreover, work for a few years and then return to law school to pursue postgraduate training in a specific area of law.

Finally, recognize the unique opportunity that law school represents. For most lawyers, the full-time practice of law requires a dedication of time that rarely permits leisurely study of broad areas of law. As a law student, you have the gift of time (to identify your interests, to gather the building-block knowledge essential to your chosen area, and to fill in the gaps in your education). Use that gift wisely.

THE SUMMER ASSOCIATE EXPERIENCE

The law firm recruiting process often gives the impression that the only thing that matters is getting a good job. Law school placement offices give students statistics about law firms (various ratings of size, salaries, profitability, and other measures). Law firms keep track of their own statistics (numbers of students from top schools, numbers of judicial clerks, and other measures). These statistics suggest that hiring is what counts and that qualitative factors (making sure that there is a good fit between a law firm's needs and opportunities and a student's talents and interests) somehow do not much matter.

On this view, the summer associate experience is essentially irrelevant. Everyone assumes that most summer associates, at most firms, will be offered jobs as permanent associates. So long as you do not make a massive blunder, you are nearly guaranteed an offer. If the goal is to get hired, and if by becoming a summer associate you are bound to be hired, there is little point in putting a lot of mental energy into the summer associate experience.

The hiring decision, however, is just an instant in a continuous process that transforms a student into a fully functioning lawyer. To be sure, getting a good job is important. But is that all there is? This section suggests some ways in which the summer associate experience can be a vital part of a law student's professional maturation.

Begin with the reality of your own previous experiences. Many law students have no practical experience in law, and many have never really spoken in depth with practicing lawyers. Reading casebooks and talking through hypotheticals in law school can help give students some concept of the practice of law. So can talking with law professors (many of whom have, or have had, active practices). So can the popular media (books, movies, and television shows). But none of these can substitute for actually doing the practical business of law. For many students, the summer associate position is the first real opportunity to use the skills and explore the interests they have been developing in law school.

Beyond this skill and aptitude testing, a summer job in a law firm may be a student's first real opportunity to spend unbounded time with practicing lawyers outside the artificial confines of classrooms and the interviewing process. Although not all lawyers will let their hair down with students, the summer associate experience generally provides a very good opportunity to ask lawyers what they think about the practice of law, about their own practice areas, about their law firm, and about their lifestyles. The opportunity to talk to all the lawyers in a firm (junior and senior), whether they are on the recruiting committee or not, may give you a much better impression of the firm than you might otherwise have.

Here, then, are some tips for making the most of your summer associate experience. These tips, of course, must be adapted to your individual situation.

Develop a Plan

Think in advance of what you would most like to get out of the summer associate experience. Is there one practice area you really want to sample? Is there a particular lawyer with whom you would like to work? Is there a kind of transaction or litigation you would like to experience? The clearer you are about your priority, the more people you tell about your plan (the recruiting director, the summer associate coordinators, and other lawyers in the firm), and the earlier you begin to tell people of your plan, the greater the likelihood that you will get what you want.

Develop a Mentor and Buddy Relationship

Many firms assign mentors (senior lawyers) and buddies (junior lawyers) to their summer associates. If you find your assigned mentor and buddy relationships satisfactory, use them. Mentors and buddies can help you formulate and implement a plan for your summer associate experience. They can also help answer your questions about the firm and other issues that matter to you (and can help direct you to others in the firm who may be able to help you). On your return to law school, moreover, mentors and buddies can be a continuing source of information for you and can be a bridge to the firm during the year(s) you have remaining in school. A mentor and a buddy may also provide continuing assistance when you return to the firm as an associate (providing a friendly face, sage advice when you need it, and entrée into the work and workings of the firm).

If your firm has no formal mentor and buddy system, make the acquisition of at least one mentor and buddy a top priority for the summer. You need not restrict yourself to just one of each, of course. Indeed, if the mentor and buddy that you are first assigned or first develop prove unhelpful, be flexible and search for others. The key is to find people who are accessible, who are willing to spend time with you, and who are easy to engage in conversation.

Get out of Your Office

There is a temptation to assume that the firm expects you to put in long hours as a summer associate to show your dedication and enterprise. For most summer jobs, however, the focus is generally more on quality than quantity of work. Again, the important point is that the summer associate experience is a unique opportunity to get to know lawyers in the firm. Although you may meet some by working with them, you will meet most lawyers at the firm in social settings.

Maximize the opportunities for such meetings. Go to the planned social events (cocktail parties, dinners, entertainment activities). At those events, do not clump with the other summer associates. Seek out a lawyer in the firm you know at least marginally. Strike up or join a conversation; ask him or her to introduce you to other lawyers in his or her circle. If you know absolutely no one at an event, introduce yourself to the nearest lawyer and proceed from there.

In general, your goal should be to let as many lawyers as possible know who you are and what your interests include. Telling lawyers about your plan for the summer and asking their opinions and advice on the plan would be a fine way to introduce yourself. Your goal should be to leave a generally favorable impression with every lawyer you meet. Expression of enthusiasm and interest in the firm and its lawyers will usually leave a favorable impression. Beyond that, you should probe for information about the firm, its lawyers, and its clients for your own purposes. The more you understand about the firm and your potential place in it, the better you will be able to make a choice for a position after law school.

Do High Quality Work at All Times

Although it may be rare for a summer associate to lose a job offer based on poor performance alone, the point of a summer associate experience is to begin your relationship with lawyers in the firm on the best possible terms. Your reputation for competence and thoroughness begins to develop as soon as you begin doing any substantive work (even the sometimes mundane research often assigned to summer associates). All the basic rules apply to summer assignments. Make sure you understand the assignment. Ask questions to clarify your understanding. Get a good sense of the deadline for the project, and how long the assigning lawyer thinks it should take. Check in periodically with the assigning lawyer to let him or her know about your progress and any problems you have encountered. Be sure to deliver the form of work product that is expected. Proofread every document and make it as good as you possibly can. Treat every assignment as a career maker. Do not overload yourself with work to the point that you cannot give your highest-quality performance to every project.

Act Like a Professional

Most law firms tolerate (and even encourage) some high-spirited merriment and hijinks among their summer associates. Nevertheless, firms are generally not willing to hire the truly immature and emotionally uncontrolled. Keep in mind that every lawyer you meet will be forming an impression of you, which may be lasting. Be careful of misusing alcohol. Be careful of making offensive racial, sexual, and other inappropriate remarks. Be careful of banter, sarcasm, and tasteless jokes that may be misinterpreted or poorly received. Act on the assumption that all your discussions with lawyers in the firm are on the record. Indeed, your encounters with these lawyers truly do build a record, which may affect your permanent offer and your future success at the firm.

Use Your New Knowledge

After spending a summer at a law firm, you may have a new appreciation and understanding of the practice of law. Build on that knowledge. For your last year(s) in law school, consider what courses you should take that might better equip you to practice at the firm. Consider also whether there are internships or part-time work that could round out your law school education with additional practical experience.

Think deeply, moreover, about your postgraduation plan. If you have confirmed your interest in continuing as a permanent associate at the firm where you summered, have you also narrowed your practice area interest? If not, formulate a plan to help gather more information and experience from which to make that decision.

If you conclude that the firm at which you summered may not be right for you, develop a plan for exploring other opportunities. Consider the parts of your summer experience that caused you to reject the firm. Are those things that can be different at another firm? What characteristics would you look for in another firm that might achieve that change? Be realistic, recognizing that some parts of the law firm experience (long hours, for example) may be inherent in most firms.

Compare Notes

Throughout your summer experience, you should talk to the other summer associates at the firm to learn what experiences they have had and what impressions they have formed. These discussions can greatly expand your base of information and understanding of the firm.

You should also speak to your fellow law students back at school, when they return from their summers at other firms. The comparison of firsthand experiences is often far superior to the general descriptions of firms found in recruiting guides or the anonymous postings on message boards about the profession.

Ultimately, the goal of this intelligence gathering is to increase your confidence that your choice of a permanent position is likely to give you a fair opportunity to be successful and satisfied. Indeed, that confidence, and the positive, forward-looking attitude that goes with it, may be one of the most important indicators of future success.

Beginning Full-Time Practice

2

OVERVIEW

You have graduated from law school. You have taken the bar examination. You are ready to start your professional career at a law firm. What do you do now? Work hard, certainly. Try to learn, of course. Gain some experience, hopefully. But to what end? What is it that you are trying to accomplish? What is the object of this game? How do you win the game?

These questions are not answered by rote. There is no single brass ring that everyone can or should reach out to grab. There are, however, some guidelines. The game is not entirely random. In fact, new lawyers have been playing this game for years. More experienced lawyers know how they survived the game. As a result of surviving the game, moreover, they have some expectations of how the next generation of lawyers should behave. It is, therefore, worth your while to study some of the rules of this game. Once you understand those rules, you can begin to refine the way you play your individual version of the game.

This overview is meant as a general introduction for new associates in law firms. It is not meant to address the circumstances of every lawyer, in every law firm, in every area of practice. Even with those limitations, there are some universal aspects of the enculturation of new lawyers. When studied and understood, these universal rules can help new lawyers mature and prosper in professional development.

Cultivate a Good Reputation

The key to professional development is reputation. Your goal, throughout your career, is to establish and enhance your reputation.

The process is never-ending. Every lawyer, every day, adds to or detracts from (in some ways) his or her reputation.

Reputation begins at the most basic level. The staff at your firm will come to think of you as a nice person, or as someone who is difficult. Your secretary will talk to other secretaries, who will form similar impressions. These impressions matter. At the crunch point (when your word processing or copying needs to get done quickly and accurately, for example), you would prefer that an ally does your work, rather than someone who does not know or care about you, or worse yet, someone who thinks you are a jerk.

Reputation quickly expands to the other lawyers for whom you work. They talk to each other. They ask who is dependable, hardworking, and capable. You want your name to be mentioned on the short list of that company.

Ultimately, reputation extends to clients. In many instances, clients have choices, even within your firm, of the lawyers doing their work. Again, if a client has a problem, you want to be mentioned as a candidate to assist in doing the work. Similarly, when a senior lawyer in your firm tells a client that you are working on a project, you should hope that the client knows that you are a valuable addition to the team, either as a result of the client's prior experience or because the senior lawyer holds you in high regard.

How do you build a good reputation? Most important is to recognize the needs of senior lawyers and clients and to match those needs against your strengths and weaknesses. If you were the lawyer who supervises your work, what are four or five things you would say are your strengths? The words may vary, but they generally should include terms like: dependable, hardworking, organized, clear thinking, careful, and enthusiastic. Notice that these terms have very little to do with the substantive knowledge you may have. Senior lawyers do not expect you to have complete mastery of subjects on which they have spent years developing expertise. They do expect you to apply yourself fully, to learn from your experiences, and to demonstrate a genuine interest in improving your skills.

On the other side of the ledger, if you were criticizing your performance, what words might you use? If the converse of any of the positive attributes just mentioned (irresponsible, lazy, sloppy, confused, careless, or lackluster) appears in your characterization, you have a reputation problem, which you need to work (very hard) at correcting.

What can you do? First, abandon any sense of entitlement to a good reputation. Your fabulous résumé got you in the door at your law firm. It matters very little thereafter. Senior lawyers and clients generally care about how you perform, not where you come from. You have to work at developing your reputation, from the ground up. It is hard work, and there will be setbacks. Do not despair. Do not ignore the task. Get going, today, and keep at it.

Second, treat every assignment as a career maker. No senior lawyer (and certainly no client) wants to think of his work as unimportant. Strive to make your work product on every task as good as it can be. Your question to yourself on any given task is "Would I stake my reputation on this work?"

Finally, look for the confluence of work you like to do and work that is likely to be valued by senior lawyers and clients. It matters little if you have a strong interest and aptitude for criminal law if your firm does no work and has no clients in that area. Conversely, it ultimately will not help you to develop a specialty that your firm considers vital if you do not enjoy the work. A good reputation is not the sole aim of your professional life. It is, however, the natural by-product of a satisfying, challenging, and active career.

Develop Repeat Business

For most new lawyers in most firms, there is some system for assigning work. Frequently, there is an assigning partner, or a new associate group coordinator, whose responsibility is to find work for you and other new associates. This person should be considered a resource, not a substitute for selling your services to senior lawyers and ultimately clients.

Your goal should be to develop repeat business in areas of practice you find interesting and with lawyers and clients you find enjoyable. A large part of the experience in the first few years of practice at a law firm involves a mutual process by which you try to find out what you like while senior lawyers and clients find out about your capabilities. You can approach the process passively or with an eye toward actively choosing your own career path.

The passive approach essentially means that someone else (usually the assigning partner or new associate coordinator) will make choices for you. That person will refer requests for assistance from senior lawyers and clients to you. In most instances, unless you have too much to do already, you will have little choice but to agree to do the work. Although the assigning lawyer probably will have some knowledge of your ability and inclination, he or she cannot possibly know as much about your likes and dislikes as you do. As a result, there will often be projects for which you feel little connection or interest. Worse yet, if you have little interest in a project, you may find yourself doing less than your best work. Your reputation, unfortunately, may suffer.

The more active approach is preferable. The essence of this approach is to recognize that you need to create a demand for your services. You need to establish yourself as a "go to" player, someone to whom senior lawyers will look to staff their projects, even if an assigning coordinator does not intervene on your behalf. The more demand there is for your services, the more you can choose the projects on which you work and the more ability you have to fend off work that you do not prefer, with the completely legitimate excuse that you are just too busy with other work.

How do you do that? In reality, this question is nothing more than "How do I build a good reputation?" There are, however, a few things that are crucial to developing repeat business. First, and this may seem ironic, work as hard as possible on tasks that you dislike. Give senior lawyers the impression that you are a "can do" person, even on mundane, boring tasks. Give them a reason to think that as they help develop your skills and allow you to work with their clients, they can expect that you will perform as well on more difficult, interesting tasks as you do on the most basic.

Second, within the area of your ability, make sure that you are adding value. When the senior lawyer says, "We need 20 copies of this document, bound, with blue covers," know precisely how to do that, with few additional questions asked. When the product comes back, make sure that it is perfect. Be a stickler for detail. Do not assume that the senior lawyer will fix a problem if you ignore it. If you are fully conversant with all the essential systems of your office (telephones, fax machines, photocopiers, computers, library), senior lawyers can count on you to "sweat the details." You will be perceived to add value to their teams, and you will more likely get repeat business.

Finally, each time you have an opportunity to say, in substance, that you like a particular kind of work or like working with a particular lawyer, say it. Say it because you mean it, of course. But say it also because it is a sure way to convey your enthusiasm and to increase the likelihood that you will get more work that you find rewarding. You can express your enthusiasm in other ways as well. When you get calls from senior lawyers who have projects or areas of practice you find interesting, run, do not walk, to their offices and offer to help in any way you can. When a senior lawyer lets you work directly with a client on a task that you find interesting, do your very best work and always ask if there is anything more you can do to help.

Treat Supervising Lawyers as Your First Clients

At the earliest stage of your career, your direct contact with clients outside the firm is likely to be limited. In effect, your clients are the senior lawyers in your firm, who, in giving you assignments, are also offering you the opportunity to try out skills that you will eventually use when working directly with clients.

One of the principal talents that clients expect in their lawyers is problem-solving ability. Clients come to their lawyers with specific problems. Generally, clients present questions about how they should best proceed in a given situation. Lawyers analyze the facts and applicable law and, using their best judgment, provide a recommended course of action. Even if the client does not accept every part of the lawyer's advice, the client will generally appreciate prompt, specific advice on how to deal with the problem.

Similarly, the new associate, confronted with a question from a senior lawyer, should view the exercise as one of problem solving. The first issue is how quickly the problem must be solved. Many assignments for new associates involve library research. Such assignments can be bounded by a specific time frame, or they can essentially be unlimited in scope. Thus, the first thing you should determine is how soon the senior lawyer wants an answer. Your awareness of the time frame should provide you with an understanding of how much detail the senior lawyer expects in response to the questions. Make every effort to abide by that time frame. Nothing can be as annoying to a senior lawyer as when an associate is given a specific research assignment with a specific time frame and does not report back prior to expiration of the deadline.

The deadline may also have a financial component. For example, the client may not wish to spend a large amount of money on researching the finer points of law surrounding the question. Under those circumstances, the senior lawyer may become particularly irritated to discover that you have spent hours of time on expensive electronic research when a 20 minute review of a major treatise would give the essential answer.

The same goes for communicating the answer. Depending on the time frame and the budget for the project, the senior lawyer may simply want an oral report that summarizes the answer. Some lawyers, however, under some circumstances may wish to have a more detailed memorandum explaining the nuances of the answer and the sources of research. In some instances, your written work may be expected to go directly into a brief. You should determine, by asking the senior lawyer in advance, what form and what length of answer is requested.

If at any point in the course of your work on a project you become uncertain about whether you are following the instructions from a senior lawyer correctly, you should not hesitate to return to the senior lawyer for further direction. If there is any way to compound the problem of spending excessive time and resources on an assignment, it is surely to produce useless work product, which the senior lawyer must simply discard. Better to make yourself something of a pest with repeated questions than to wander aimlessly around a problem that you do not fully understand. Most senior lawyers are aware that the complicated legal problems they often confront require a certain amount of direction and supervision to answer properly. Indeed, most senior lawyers will give you credit for checking to make sure that you are following their directions.

As you become familiar with the working style of the senior lawyers in your firm, you will become more confident in going back to them for advice at critical junctures in the course of a project. This is the essence of the professional development process. As you gain experience, moreover, you will become ever more aware of the importance of consultation with fellow lawyers and clients on key points of strategy.

Earn the Right to Choose Your Work

Your skills when you arrive at your new firm are most likely very generalized. Even though law school may have involved specific substantive courses, in large measure what you bring to the firm at the earliest point is the ability to research, write, and spend long hours reviewing documents. Part of the process of assimilation at the firm is a demonstration of your willingness to perform even these mundane tasks.

Your goal, however, is to demonstrate to senior lawyers that you are interested in learning the practical aspects of practice in a particular area. Assuming that you have such an interest, there are several different ways to demonstrate that you are ready to move on to more substantive work.

First, as previously mentioned, you should be as direct as possible in telling senior attorneys where your interests lie. When you work on a project that you find rewarding, tell the senior lawyer precisely that. Second, even if you are assigned mundane tasks, if you find the area of the project or case interesting, do not confine yourself to the mundane. Even if the work cannot be billed to a client, for example, you may want to do some extracurricular reading of treatises, practice primers, or journals in the area of the project. As you learn about the background of the project, you may also want to do some extracurricular reading pertaining to the particular client. All this work will help you to have broader and more productive discussion with senior lawyers concerning the project and the substantive area. As they begin to see you as a knowledgeable and enthusiastic colleague, they will more likely share their experience in the substantive area and with the particular client. Your knowledge, experience and confidence will further grow.

Another effective way to demonstrate enthusiasm and approximate the role of the senior lawyers to which you aspire is to formulate solutions to the problems confronting senior lawyers. That is, as you understand the project or problem presented by the client, think about what solution you would recommend if you were the senior attorney. By discussing the proposed solution with the senior attorney, if you have done your homework, you may find that your ideas are helpful to the senior lawyer. Even if they are not, the fact that you have attempted to come up with an answer may impress the senior lawyer with your enthusiasm and dedication. Ultimately, your goal is to have the senior lawyer view you as a person who is worth investing some amount of time in for training and promoting so that you can assist in future projects more effectively and independently.

Become a Valued Team Member

A large part of the professional process at major law firms is the creation of practice teams for particular substantive areas and for particular cases or projects. As a new associate, your goal should be to determine which of these teams involve areas of practice and lawyers in which you are interested.

This focus on teams may be foreign to your experience from law school and even from summer associate experiences. Law school courses lack continuity, in the sense that courses have beginning and ending points. The same is true for summer associates, who are at the firm for a limited period of time and are typically given work assignments (like library research) that are limited in scope and essentially individual rather than part of a team experience.

When you arrive at a firm on a permanent basis, however, the more complete professional assimilation process begins. Despite the large number of lawyers in this country and perhaps in the metropolitan area where you work, in reality you probably will deal with only a small number of lawyers at your firm. Depending on your practice area, even your local legal community may be small. This focus on practice teams and community should reinforce the notion of reputation as a critical element for success. Your goal is to become a valued member on each practice team to which you belong. As senior lawyers and clients form new practice teams for new assignments, your goal is to be a valued addition to any such team.

Despite your junior status, moreover, senior lawyers and clients will respect your demonstrated ability to assemble and effectively manage a team of administrative staff, such as secretaries and paralegals. The more you demonstrate your ability to pay attention to details and take whatever steps are necessary to complete the project effectively and on time, the more likely senior lawyers and clients will want to add you to their practice teams.

Make "Face Time" with Supervising Lawyers

The opposite of team participation, of course, is isolation. Unfortunately, the great temptation when you get to a new firm is to spend too much of your time in your individual office. You may think that staying in your office gives other lawyers the impression that you are hard working. You may also simply be intimidated by the senior lawyers walking the halls. You may even think that by staying in your office, you can avoid being noticed and avoid undesirable work. All these are false assumptions.

Your goal should be, as much as possible, to have direct face-to-face communication with as many senior lawyers and clients as possible, especially those involved in practice areas and projects of interest to you. You should make it a priority to spend some part of every day outside your office. If that involves nothing more than a quick walk around the halls of your firm, so be it. The great likelihood is that somewhere in the process of such a stroll you will encounter a senior lawyer with whom you are working. These encounters offer opportunities to discuss the status of any projects on which you are working. Such encounters can help keep senior lawyers aware of your work and help convince them of your enthusiasm and interest in their work.

Similarly, when you get a phone call from senior attorneys asking you to come to their offices to discuss a project, do not hesitate to do so. Always bring along a pad and pencil to write down any significant facts gained in the discussion and to make note of any assignments that the senior attorney may give you.

You should also expect that any discussion with a senior attorney may be interrupted by phone calls or visits from other lawyers or even clients. Do not leave the office of the senior attorney until you are told to do so. During the downtime in the course of a meeting with a senior attorney, do something productive. Many new associates routinely bring extra work or reading material with them when they go to a senior lawyer's office. If it does not involve intrusion on the senior lawyer's privacy, moreover, you should listen carefully to how the senior lawyer deals with other lawyers and clients. As you learn what is standard practice for a senior attorney, you may also want to spend some time studying the contents of the senior lawyer's office. Take a look at the books the lawyer has in the practice area in which you are interested. You may want to consider getting copies of these books for your extracurricular reading. You may also want to note the senior lawyer's social interests, often reflected in pictures of family, awards, and other memorabilia displayed about the office. Again, the more interest you show in other lawyers and clients, the more likely they will respond to you and help you to learn and foster your career.

Conversely, you should take every precaution not to become known as a "stealth" associate. When you have completed an assignment for a senior attorney, call the attorney to find out when you can best come by to report on your progress. Do not simply leave results of your work on a lawyer's desk or chair. The face-to-face meeting with a senior lawyer is a critical opportunity to demonstrate your interest in the project and to correct any mistakes that may have occurred in the course of your work. Indeed, this may be the only opportunity you have to solicit vital feedback on your progress.

Take Responsibility for Your Mistakes

Everyone makes mistakes. Your goal as a new associate is to recognize your mistakes as early as possible and to correct them before they become larger problems. Do not run away from your mistakes, and do not blame others for your mistakes. View your mistakes as what they can be in the way of learning opportunities.

Remember also that senior attorneys may judge you more by your reaction to the mistakes than by the mistakes themselves. If you try to run away from mistakes or to blame others for them, senior attorneys will get the impression that you are not trustworthy and not a team player. Ultimately, senior attorneys expect you to take responsibility for your mistakes because that is what they must do in their own professional lives. Indeed, if you become part of the management structure of a team, you are responsible for helping to prevent and manage any mistakes made by anyone on the team. Thus, just as senior lawyers must take responsibility for their failure to prevent you from making mistakes, so too, you must take responsibility for preventing and rectifying mistakes by your subordinates, including secretaries, paralegals, and other staff.

Demonstrate Professional Courtesy

You are being paid a substantial sum of money to perform professional tasks as an attorney. Your goal should be to earn your pay by becoming as professionally competent and effective as you can be. Professional competence means more than simply getting a job done. Professional competence means viewing the interest of your firm as paramount. In particular, professionalism means valuing courtesy and group development over individual competition.

Law school often fosters a measure of cutthroat competition. Effective professional development requires that you temper your competitive instincts with the recognition that you are part of an organization composed of real human beings with real human needs. When you see one of your colleagues with a time crunch or a personal problem, it is your professional obligation to step in to help if you can. Similarly, if you see a subordinate attorney, paralegal, secretary, or staff member who has made a mistake, it is your professional obligation to help correct the mistake and to prevent it from happening again without abusing the subordinate in the process.

Respect Deadlines

A key aspect of your reputation is the extent to which you are perceived as reliable. As you become part of a practice team, senior attorneys and clients will come to expect you to perform critical tasks aimed at helping solve their problems. Your goal is to set reasonable expectations for such performance and to meet or exceed such expectations on a regular basis.

In that connection, one essential part of your professional development should be establishment of a reliable calendar of your business and personal activities. If a senior lawyer or client asks you to meet a specific deadline for completing a task, you need to be able to evaluate the extent of the demand being made on your time and determine whether that deadline is reasonable. You also need to be able to evaluate any resource constraints that may limit your ability to perform the task on time. Ultimately, part of the judgment for which clients and senior lawyers value your services is the ability to look ahead at the steps required to complete a project and to anticipate potential problems and ensure that the necessary steps are completed in a timely fashion.

Communicate

If you wish to be part of a team, you need to make sure that you are in regular communication with other members of the team. If you are going to be away from your office and out of communication even for a short period of time, there should be some way for senior lawyers and clients to find you. In general, all you need to do is keep your secretary informed of your location and your schedule. Similarly, if you leave a telephone message with a senior lawyer or client, make sure to leave your telephone number and note any extended period when you will not be available to take a return call. If you will be unavailable for a period of time, you also should make sure to inform senior lawyers of your absence, and make sure that a replacement attorney is taking responsibility for any task assigned to you and that he or she knows how to communicate with you while you are away.

Communication also means that whenever you find that two projects impose conflicting demands on your time, you keep track of the conflicts and inform senior lawyers and clients about your time constraints. You are responsible for letting your supervising attorneys know of any such constraints.

Seek Opportunities for Professional Growth

Part of the process of professional growth is seeking out, wherever possible, practical experiences in your chosen substantive area of practice. In a litigation context, for example, writing a section of a brief is generally preferable to writing an office memorandum because the brief-writing experience is closer to the practical problem. On that same view, writing the entire brief is preferable to writing a section, and arguing the motion as well as writing the brief is even further along the path of skill development.

These practical experiences should be a critical part of your own measure of your experience at your firm. These experiences will also be a measure by which you are judged by senior attorneys and clients. That is, the more that senior attorneys and clients see that you are capable of performing more demanding tasks, the more likely it is that you will get interesting and challenging work.

Not all your experiences will involve progress in your skill set. You need to be aware that even modest expansion of your experience is desirable for a new associate. At very least, the issue deserves your attention. You can and should develop your own personal measure of your experiences. How many strategy meetings have you participated in with senior lawyers? How many meetings with clients? How many meetings outside of your office? With litigators, how many experiences in court? How many evidentiary hearings or trials? All these are learning opportunities, and your goal should be to have as many as possible.

Again, the essential part of your strategy is to convince senior lawyers and clients that you can add value in a situation. Even if it involves carrying the bags, arranging for transportation, booking a conference room, setting up a teleconference, getting copies made, finding lunch, or other mundane tasks, you should grab for any opportunity to be of service in order to justify your participation in these experiences and to maximize the chances that you will have further growth opportunities.

A word about notes. In most settings, even if you are not conducting a meeting or participating in a court proceeding directly, you can serve a valid function as a note-taker. Unless you are told not to do so by a senior lawyer or client, you should assign yourself the task of note-taking in any such setting. After any such meeting or proceeding, you should ask the senior lawyer and client whether they would like a written summary of the events for their files.

You should also recognize that your role may include contacts with people outside the firm, including clients, lawyers, judges, and their staffs. Part of your function is to serve as a representative of the firm. You should always view your role as demonstrating the professional competence and integrity of the firm.

Let Your Office Help You

As a new associate, you will spend an enormous amount of time in your office. You should view your office as a tool for organizing critical information that you will use in your daily practice. It is also a tool for communicating with senior lawyers and clients who come in contact with you.

Begin by developing some form of filing system. You do not want to have piles of papers strewn about your office. In such an environment, your secretary would never be able to help organize your materials. Senior lawyers will never be able to find materials in your office in your absence. The impression that your office conveys, moreover, will be one of disorganization. Given your junior status, of course, you want to convey precisely the opposite message. Senior lawyers and clients may count on you to keep materials organized so that they can focus on the more significant aspects of the case or project.

Your office, however, can and should be an extension of your own personality. You should feel free to decorate your office with items of personal interest. The impression such decoration gives senior lawyers and clients is that you are more than a temporary visitor at the firm. You will appear to be someone who is comfortable in the firm setting and who intends to grow and flourish in that setting.

You should spend some time accumulating a library of critical volumes in your practice area, with emphasis on books that you frequently refer to in doing research in the library. These are candidates for inclusion in your private library. Such materials can help you practice more efficiently, and their appearance on book shelves in your office gives the impression to senior lawyers and clients that you have dedicated yourself to mastering your chosen practice area.

Get a Life

Your life as a lawyer should involve more than work. Indeed, part of the process of developing as an attorney is learning how to manage your time outside the office. Clients and senior lawyers will relate to you better if you have some sense of the world beyond the walls of your firm. You also need some ability to manage the stress and long hours of professional life.

Being a professional also means having some personal interest in the lives and problems of your colleagues and clients. You will find that most people mix discussion of their business problems with their personal experiences. Showing some interest in both aspects will often be a critical part of developing professional relationships.

Perhaps the prototypical example of such a discussion is the evening meal following a business meeting in some distant spot. There you sit with senior lawyer, client, or both. Are you enough of a conversationalist to be engaging throughout the meal? If not, you may find that your professional relationships suffer.

Relax

Your first years in professional life are certainly important. They are, however, only the starting point. The process of professional development is just that, a process, and it takes time.

Although you should always try your hardest, recognize that no single project, and no single mistake, will make or break your career. Do not become discouraged if there are setbacks along the road. Just as the dieter should not give up dieting because he has fallen prey to some tempting morsels at a single dinner, so too, you should not be diverted from your planned development, even if it is not always smooth, and your progress not immediately apparent.

Indeed, in the often highly charged atmosphere of a busy law firm, any feedback (let alone positive feedback) from supervising lawyers is often sorely lacking. Solicit feedback where you can. If it does not come, however, mark your own progress. Talk to your fellow new associates. Share experiences so that the group as a whole can develop.

Above all else, be a good friend to yourself. When you succeed, celebrate. When there are setbacks, console yourself, and take action to try to avoid the problem in the future.

THE IMPORTANCE OF DETAILS

Most law students are conditioned to inquire, during the law firm interviewing process, whether the firm will give a junior lawyer lots of responsibility early on in his or her career. Law firm recruiters expect this inquiry and are generally conditioned to assure law students that the firm will give them plenty of immediate responsibility.

But what is the nature of that immediate responsibility? The truth, of course, is that junior lawyers are often responsible, at the beginning of their careers, for handling the most mundane aspects of most projects. Awareness of that fact, however, need not be cause for dismay. The junior lawyer who learns to sweat the details on a project is well on the way to becoming a fully functioning lawyer, capable of exercising much more responsibility. This section suggests some of the steps along that path.

Learn the Process

The case method of study in law school focuses largely on only one level of practice in the law, the creation of judicial opinions (mostly at the appellate level). Vast areas of the practice of law (not the black letter substantive rules, but how things get done) are omitted in a classic law school education.

The result is that, although most newly minted lawyers know how to do legal research and how to write an office memorandum, they know little about how to do most essential tasks in a law firm (in litigation, for example, how to write or answer a complaint, how to prepare a motion, how to take a deposition, how to settle a case, or how to prepare for trial). For junior corporate and commercial lawyers, moreover, although they may have taken courses in corporations, securities law, and the like, most law students do not learn how to negotiate a deal, conduct due diligence, or complete a closing.

The aim of the most junior lawyer, therefore, need not be to begin to do all these things immediately. Instead, the first aim should be to learn as much as possible of the process of how a litigation or a deal gets done. Part of that learning, to be sure, comes from doing real work on real projects in a law firm. But the junior lawyer should also seek out nonbillable experiences and education that can help in the learning process. Many firms offer in-house seminars that aim at imparting this kind of information. Bar associations and continuing legal education groups also often offer practical introductions for the new lawyer. You may also find that an inquiry of a senior lawyer in your practice area will turn up his or her favorite introductory text or practical guide to work in your area. Borrow the book, read it, and (if you find it useful) get your own copy for future reference.

Learn the Forms

Virtually every practice area has some basic forms that are used repeatedly. Get to know these forms, and work on creating a set of your own forms, which you will maintain for future use.

Getting to know the forms in your practice area, however, involves much more than simply having documents that can be copied and applied to different tasks. Read the documents. Read them closely. Try to understand what purposes they serve and what rules may affect their content. When you have questions about the forms (and there should be many), ask them (of your mentor, if you have one, or of the more senior associates on your teams). The forms may help you greatly (in terms of efficiency), but if you do not understand them, they can harm you greatly as well (when a form, or section of a form meant for a specific purpose, turns out to be ill-suited to the specific task at hand).

Learn the Problems

For any area of practice there are some standard projects and some standard tasks that must be performed in connection with those projects. There are also, generally, some classic problems that arise in connection with these projects. Learn to anticipate the problems in the projects in your practice area, and to formulate solutions to those problems, before they become overwhelming.

Many classic problems have to do with time: the affidavit that must be signed in time to be filed with a motion; the authorization that must be delivered in time to complete a closing; and other regular, predictable time crunches. Most effective lawyers develop time-management habits, thinking in advance about steps that must be performed and what to do if deadlines cannot be met with conventional efforts. Many lawyers, for example, routinely make contingency plans for how to deliver a document after normal business hours, or arrange for multiple methods of delivery of the same document, to ensure that it arrives when required.

In the same way, there are some classic problems of organization on most projects. Most experienced lawyers are well aware that failure to organize materials and information at the outset of a project can lead to chaos and inefficiency as the project progresses. Effective junior lawyers think of organizational schemes (filing systems, lists of tasks in progress, contact lists, and the like) that can make work on the project much easier for everyone.

Learn to Be Helpful

The law school setting fools some law students into thinking that every person can act independently in the law. You read the book; you go to the lectures; you do the outline; you take the test; it's over. The law firm setting is often the precise opposite; the key to your success is the extent to which you are perceived as being helpful to others. You may have a brilliant legal mind, but if you cannot provide effective service on the projects at your firm, you will not be well regarded.

On every new project with which you become involved, think of all the things you could do that might be helpful to the senior lawyers and client involved in the project, then ask the more senior lawyers (repeatedly) whether they want you to perform any of these tasks. Many of these tasks may be the standard forms of research to which you are accustomed: "Do you want me to check on the elements of that cause of action?" "Do you need to know what the filing requirements are under Delaware law?" Others, however, may be the much more mundane tasks of getting a project done: "Do you need to get a conference room for that meeting?" "Do you want me to arrange for overtime word processing?"

Be mindful, moreover, of the help you can provide just by being well organized. On virtually every project, for example, there will come a time when a senior lawyer will ask you to retrieve an important document, even though the document surely exists somewhere in the senior lawyer's office or files. Similarly, in many instances, the most junior members of a team pay the most attention to schedules and deadlines, reminding senior lawyers and clients of when things have to be done. By being super-organized and by taking responsibility for paying attention to these kinds of details, you demonstrate to senior lawyers and clients your dedication to getting the job done right.

Learn to Pass on Your Knowledge

Your passage from law student to fully functioning junior lawyer may be quite rapid. Sooner than you may have expected, you will find yourself supervising junior lawyers, summer associates, paralegals, and others. Take advantage of these first opportunities to pass on some of what you have learned about the processes, the forms, the problems, and the organizing tricks involved in operating effectively as a junior lawyer. This teaching will come back to benefit you in many ways.

Having junior lawyers and others who know how to help you sweat the details on your projects can extend your effectiveness. Most junior lawyers, moreover, will appreciate the time you take to show them the ropes. Ultimately, the creation of an atmosphere of mutual learning and support will benefit your practice group and the firm as a whole.

SEARCHING FOR WORK ASSIGNMENTS

The summer associate experience at most law firms generally parallels the experiences that law students have accumulated over the course of an academic career. Someone develops an assignment, puts parameters on it, and hands it to you with directions on when and how to complete the assignment. The assignment lasts a week or two, and then you are done; you move on to another assignment, often in a new area, with entirely different lawyers.

The experience as a new associate at a law firm can be jarring in its difference from your summer associate and academic experiences. The spoon-feeding assignment model is rarely followed. Instead, to greater and lesser degrees, new associates are left to discover for themselves what work is available in the firm, what work is desirable (and interesting) to the particular new associate, and how to get such work. This section aims to provide some introductory advice on how to approach the task of searching for work as a new associate.

Begin with some study of the assignment system in your firm (and, in particular, your office in your firm). These systems may be arrayed on a continuum, depending on the degree of formal supervision of the assignment process. In the free market system, new associates are eligible for work from any group and any lawyer. There may be no formal coordinator of work assignments and little or no effort to keep track of what experiences you are gathering. Yet, even in this system, senior lawyers may quickly come to identify you with a particular practice area, and some of them will begin to think of you as on their teams for particular projects.

In an assisted assignment system, there will be some assignment coordinator, for the new associates as a whole, or for the individual practice groups. You may be required to choose a particular practice group before you start work at the firm, or you may follow some form of rotation through practice groups for a period of time, or you may be eligible for any assignment from any group. The assignment coordinators often assist in getting new lawyers their initial assignments, and in ensuring that your practice experiences generally meet your expectations. Over time, however, the formal role of the assignment coordinators becomes less and less important. As in a free market system, over time you will become identified with a particular group, and one or more practice teams, and you will begin to take more assignments informally than you do through the coordinators.

Finally, in the so-called "ball and chain" system, you may be assigned to one particular senior lawyer or practice team from the outset. That lawyer or team will generally be responsible for keeping you occupied. If you are not fully occupied or if you have an interest in working in another area or on another practice team, however, you may still need to search for work on your own.

Thus, no matter what the system, an element of individual initiative will be important as you seek to find work that is rewarding and interesting and to develop the skills and contacts within the firm that will affect your developing status. No matter what particular assignment system you encounter, moreover, the assignment process will be much less formal than you are used to from law school and the summer associate experience.

The full-time practice of law, for most lawyers, brings work in irregular waves. There is rarely a neatly ordered assembly line of projects that follows a steady, predictable pace. Instead, most lawyers can be extremely busy at times, but can have quite slack periods at other times. For new lawyers, learning to deal with the ups and downs of practice can be a large part of the initial challenge.

The goal for new associates is generally to develop stable relationships with enough lawyers and practice teams to produce a steady diet of worthwhile work.

There are several points to keep in mind as you go about searching for steady, rewarding, and interesting work:

- Unless you are told definitively the limits of a project, you will generally be eligible for more work than just the first thing you are asked to do on a project. Indeed, if you do a good job on the first assignment, you can expect to be called back for additional work (on the same project and sometimes on entirely unrelated matters).

- You are generally entitled to inquire of supervising lawyers whether they have additional work for you. Often, this kind of inquiry can be built into the ongoing process of work on a project. If you express enthusiasm for the work and indicate that you would like to do more (on this particular project, on similar projects, or more generally in this practice group and for this lawyer), you can usually expect a positive response and (sooner or later) more work.

- It is often extremely difficult to predict when additional work will arise. Even senior lawyers may not be able to predict when and how client needs will develop. Many senior lawyers, moreover, may be so caught up in their own work that they fail to spend time charting out their needs for subordinate support on a project (at least not until the need becomes urgent). The only good solution from a junior lawyer's perspective is to inquire, frequently, about the status of a senior lawyer's projects and to ask about the possibility of getting further work. Although it may appear, at times, that a senior lawyer is annoyed at interruptions, generally the more frequently you give opportunities to a senior lawyer to assign you more work, the greater the likelihood that on one such occasion a need will be identified. Thus, keep the contacts frequent but brief.

- Beware vague promises of work that may come in at some later date. Senior lawyers may want to reserve your time for a project that ultimately never materializes. Again, the solution is communication. If you check in frequently, you may get updates on the status of potential work, and you may be able to tell a senior lawyer about your own schedule of other work. If the worst happens, and you take work for another lawyer that precludes you from doing the work of the first lawyer (when it finally comes in), you will avoid disappointment and frustration for the first lawyer if you have already told him or her that you took on a competing project.

- Beware also vague understandings as to whether your work on what is obviously a megaproject (an extremely large, long-term case or deal) will be confining in some way. Obviously, such work can be very rewarding (in terms of quality of experience, raising your profile in the firm, and meeting a large group of lawyers and businesspeople). The point, however, is that such work generally involves a commitment to work more or less exclusively on the megaproject. If you do not wish to make such a commitment, say so, or at least state as clearly as possible at the outset that you wish to work on other matters in addition to the megaproject. Do not rely on the vain hope that senior lawyers, months later, once they come to depend on you for work on the megaproject, will feel a lot of sympathy for your cries that you are not getting enough diversity of experience.

These basic realities should be considered before you start your campaign in looking for work. The form of the campaign, moreover, should also be considered. One basic strategy is to identify lawyers in your firm or office with whom you would like to work. You may get some ideas on that score from a number of sources. The firm may have a directory or promotional materials that describe the practices of particular lawyers. You may also chat with junior lawyers who are one to two years ahead of you, who will generally have a good concept of who does what work. These slightly more senior lawyers will often be more approachable than the most senior lawyers themselves. Indeed, when you are assigned to a practice team, you will often find yourself reporting to another junior lawyer, even though technically the team is run by more senior lawyers with whom you really want to work. That fact should not be disheartening. In due time, you will make contact with the team leaders, and you will eventually work much more closely with them.

Another approach in searching for work is to find at least one senior lawyer who can take your part in helping you make contacts in the areas of practice that interest you. Some firms have assignment coordinators or a formal mentoring program for this purpose (among others). Even if there is no formal system, you can follow this approach in other ways. You might "luck into" such a relationship simply by working, early on, for a senior lawyer who befriends you. Not trusting to luck, however, you might simply take whatever opportunity (at a reception, at a firm training program, even in the halls) to introduce yourself to senior lawyers with whom you would like to work and say something like: "I am very interested in your work. I would like to work with you some time." Many senior lawyers would be flattered at such an approach. Others, admittedly, might be put off. To ensure success, you might again do some reconnaissance with some of your slightly more experienced compatriots, who may have some experience with, and insights into, the personalities of senior lawyers in the firm.

Whatever campaign you choose, it is far preferable to begin thinking early about searching for work than it is to wait and hope that opportunities will be heaped on you, beyond the first few months of your experience. Savvy new associates learn to plan future assignments on a continuous basis, so that when one project ends, another is just beginning. They also do not shy away from working on two projects (or more) at once, if that is possible. In these ways, they ensure not only that they keep busy, but they also maximize their opportunities to make contacts in the firm, and to gather broad experiences, that will mark them for advancement.

Indeed, the perception that a junior lawyer is busy and "in demand" may be an important element for long-term success. By keeping a steady flow of work coming your way, you enhance your reputation within the firm, your office, and your practice groups as a valuable "go to" resource.

EXPANDING YOUR RESPONSIBILITIES

For many junior lawyers, there is a temptation to assume that all that is necessary for success in a law firm is to bill thousands of hours and to do whatever the partners tell you to do. On this view, working in a law firm is essentially no different from working in a factory or a fast-food restaurant. On a long-term basis, however, assumption of the order-taker role is no guarantee of success. Indeed, long-term success in a law firm demands much more. This section charts some of the milestones of progress in assuming the responsibilities of a fully functioning senior lawyer.

From Law School to Practice

Law school, in some ways, contributes greatly to the false assumption that order-takers can be successful in the legal profession. Law school sets a method of study (casebooks, Socratic lectures, final examinations) that is easy to understand and that essentially cannot be modified by the individual student. Success, in the general sense of good grades, in the law school setting can be achieved largely by raw intellect and hard work alone. Moreover, lack of success in one class generally does not affect the remainder of a student's law school career. With blind grading, each test is independent of the others, and a reputation for excellence, to the extent that it matters at all in law school, depends mostly on cumulative grades rather than word of mouth from one professor to the next.

The practice of law in a firm changes most of the rules that law students understand. Once a student gets a job, the principal sources of his or her prior professional self-esteem (quality of law school, grade point average, quality of student journal) essentially become, at best, background facts. Most senior lawyers (and most clients) care how well you perform, not where you went to school, or how well you did. When a junior lawyer makes a serious mistake, moreover, most senior lawyers and clients will not brush it off with anything like "Well, she messed up my project, but she did make law review at a great law school, so that's okay."

Unlike law school, with its standard format of book, lecture, and test, projects in a law firm can be highly variable. To be sure, there are some familiar tasks (research, cite-checking, the office memorandum), but there may be many other tasks for which law school provides little preparation (in business practice: due diligence, document drafting and closing; in litigation: drafting pleadings, document production, and case investigation; among many others).

Often, moreover, these assignments come in an atmosphere of seeming chaos. Senior lawyers may be too busy to tell juniors much about the background of a project, and often junior lawyers are asked to pitch in at the last minute (and sometimes at quite late hours). In addition, senior lawyers can be quirky and demanding; learning to please them is a task in itself.

Learning to Plan and to Anticipate Problems

Once the first year or so passes, most junior lawyers have a better concept of how a law firm works and have a grounding in some of the basic skills of practice. At this point, a senior lawyer can assign a basic task and expect it to be done with relatively little supervision.

Yet, the junior associate remains largely an order-taker, waiting for and then implementing the directions of senior lawyers (and, eventually, clients). The breakout point comes when the junior lawyer begins to see patterns in assignments, recognizing the steps that are usually taken on certain types of projects, and anticipating problems that commonly occur.

Indeed, the ability to "look around the corners" may become one of the most important differentiators of effective junior associates. Well-organized associates keep lists (mental, at least, and preferably written) of the steps that must be taken to complete a project, the dates by which each of the critical steps must be accomplished, and who is doing what on the project. They also recognize potential problems that may delay or sidetrack a project, and they regularly feed back progress reports to senior lawyers and clients.

Suggesting Solutions

Growth out of the order-taker role involves more than simply anticipating problems in projects, however. With experience, it is hoped, comes insight and the ability to develop solutions to problems. Thus, senior lawyers (and clients) expect junior lawyers to identify solutions and to provide them with reasonable alternatives from which to choose.

Increasingly, moreover, senior lawyers and clients expect more than just a laundry list of steps that could be taken in any given circumstance. There are many two-handed lawyers in the world ("on the one hand, you could do X; on the other hand you could do Y"). Senior lawyers and clients increasingly seek one-handed assistance: Even though you may identify alternatives, you apply your best legal and business judgment to recommend what you think should be done in the particular situation.

Personal Involvement

Ultimately, the paid problem-solver is just a hired gun. Even though you may anticipate problems on a project, suggest solutions, or even take full responsibility for completion of a project, the project assignment comes from the senior lawyer or client and is shaped largely by their directions. Your relationship is, to put it in a single word, professional.

Yet, there is still more possible. Senior lawyers and clients live their lives in many settings and in many roles for which you may be able to provide assistance. Confining yourself to a simple professional relationship may mean that these other aspects of potential relationships with them are omitted. For example, senior lawyers and clients have management responsibilities at the firm or their business for which you may not be expressly asked to provide professional advice. Yet, if you express an interest in these other management responsibilities, you may learn more of what other concerns and problems occupy their thoughts. You will better understand the priority of the projects for which you provide assistance, and you may have their thanks for your help in lightening their load.

A genuine personal interest in, and willingness to listen to, senior lawyers and clients may also help you through the transitions in their lives. Individuals may move from one law firm, business, or department to another. If you are personally involved with them, they may have a powerful incentive to remain connected to you after they move, thus preserving (and potentially extending) a valuable relationship.

Ultimately, moreover, with some senior lawyers and clients, a very close relationship may develop. Although this relationship may be based on professional interaction, it extends into so many other areas (personal, family, social) that you may come to be considered a trusted confidante. At this point, although ethical rules must be observed, the line between client and friend is almost nonexistent.

Changes Ahead

The descriptions of the types of relationships just outlined suggest neat categories. In reality, every lawyer serves in a variety of roles throughout a career. Even as you mature as a lawyer, in dealing with any new senior lawyer or client, the first interactions may confine you to the order-taker role. Even the most longstanding relationships, moreover, do not always progress to a confidante relationship. Yet, it is the aspiration to make more of professional relationships, where possible, that can help guide you through a legal career. The satisfaction that comes from performing at the highest levels of trust and confidence may be one of the most important rewards of service as a lawyer.

DEALING WITH PROBLEMS

Medical school teaches doctors how to have some of the difficult conversations that can occur in practice: telling a patient that he has a terminal illness, for example; or telling a relative that her loved one has passed away. Law school has no equivalent training in bedside manner, and yet lawyers are forced to deliver bad news on a near-daily basis as part of their practice. Clients must be told of results in cases that do not match their expectations; they must hear of problems in deals and projects entrusted to their counsel; they must learn of bills that exceed estimates. These and many more are the kinds of bad news that lawyers must be prepared to deliver.

Even at the junior level, bad things happen, and senior lawyers and clients must be told. Projects are delayed; mistakes are made; adverse developments are uncovered. The bad news must be conveyed, but how? This section outlines a few of the most important elements to consider when delivering bad news.

The Direct Approach

It is the rare circumstance where bad news improves with age. In most cases, failure to deliver bad news promptly creates a second set of problems, which can make a difficult conversation even worse. The client or senior lawyer will almost inevitably ask, in addition to questions about the bad news itself, "Why didn't you tell me earlier?" Thus, as a general rule, prompt disclosure is a must.

In conducting a bad news conversation, moreover, there is no substitute for the direct approach. Telling a client or senior lawyer up front and in the clearest terms possible what the bad news is will avoid the confusion that can result from many other less direct approaches.

- Waiting until the end of a conversation to deliver bad news mimics (at least in part) the effects of delay in having any conversation about bad news. A conversation that is otherwise normal can take a decidedly negative tone when bad news is suddenly injected, as if an afterthought. Raising the problem up front in the conversation avoids the nasty surprise, or (perhaps worse) the frantic scramble to break the bad news at a point when the client or senior lawyer needs to end the conversation to deal with other matters.
- Sugarcoating bad news ("It's really not so bad" or "You don't really have to worry about this") risks confusion. If the problem is significant enough for you to raise it, then you must have made the judgment that it is, in fact, bad news. Playing down the significance of the news sends a mixed signal. Far better to state the facts regarding the bad news and let the client or senior lawyer make his or her own judgment about how bad the news really is. (Of course, it is perfectly appropriate to deliver bad news and then say what, if anything, can be done to deal with it.)
- Asking the client or senior lawyer, indirectly, how she thinks things are going, without mentioning the bad news, to "test the waters," again may produce confusion, or avoid the issue. It is appropriate to ask for the client or senior lawyer's reaction to your news, but that assumes that you have made genuine disclosure on the issue so that the reaction is well-informed.

Discussion of Options

In some instances, bad news is final; there is nothing that you or the client or senior lawyer can do to affect the outcome. When a jury delivers an adverse verdict, for example, there is no way to go back and retry the case (although there may be other options, such as posttrial motions and appeal). The client or senior lawyer needs to know, up front and early, whether the problem is irreversible.

In most instances, however, no matter how dire the news, there will be some options available for a response to the bad news. A large part of preparing to deliver bad news involves thinking through those options.

- At a minimum, consider what steps, if any, you personally might take to respond to the problem. Most clients and senior lawyers will be very receptive to a discussion of how you plan to respond. Indeed, in some circumstances, where the solution is very obvious, and you know that no direction is required for you to proceed, it may be possible to implement a solution even before you deliver the bad news. This possibility, however, should not become an excuse for failure to make early disclosure of the problem. You may compound bad news greatly by failing to disclose the problem to the client or senior lawyer, in the hope that your solution will make the problem go away. If your solution fails, then you will have to explain not only why you failed to disclose the problem, but why you failed to tell the client or senior lawyer what you planned to do about it.

- Consider also what options you would recommend to the client or senior lawyer to deal with the bad news. A conversation that starts "There is a problem, here's what is; and here's what I think can be done about it" will generally move in a more positive direction than a conversation that sounds something like "There is a problem; what are you going to do about it?"

Prepare for the Reaction

A client or senior lawyer may have a very wide range of reactions to bad news. Failure to consider the possible reactions may make it more difficult to deliver bad news effectively.

- Do not assume that there will be an extremely negative reaction. Most clients and senior lawyers are experienced enough to have heard bad news before. Most, when confronted with bad news, will have a businesslike, professional reaction. The false assumption that there will be an extremely negative reaction may make it more difficult for you to deliver the news. Indeed, fear of negative reaction can lead to the cardinal error in delivering bad news: delay. Face your fears; put them to use in helping to make sure that you prepare a clear, understandable message about the problem; and deliver the message promptly.

- Do not assume that there will be understanding of the news. The level of sophistication and involvement of clients and senior lawyers may vary greatly. Some may have difficulty understanding the substance of the news and its implications. It is your job to make sure that the news is well understood. Often, asking questions of the client or senior lawyer regarding reactions to the news (and regarding options for a response) will help you to confirm whether your news has been understood.

- Do not assume that the client or senior lawyer will accept the news or your recommendations for a response. Emotional (even quite irrational) responses are possible. One common reaction (for extremely bad news, in particular) is a kind of numbness or denial. The news may be so startling that you must give the person some time to absorb it before you go on to discuss options and strategy. There is also the possibility of an emotional flare-up in response. Again, time may be required to permit the reaction to pass before moving on to further stages of discussion.

Some expression of sympathy for an emotional reaction may also be appropriate. The news is bad, and you both know it; it is perfectly natural to be unhappy or upset in the situation. And yet, despite the mood, you must both carry on. And you have suggestions for how to respond. Most clients and senior lawyers will appreciate messages along these lines.

At the very least, in these circumstances, you will get some credit for displaying a professional, yet caring, attitude. Indeed, some of the strongest relationships are formed in the course of dealing with adverse developments and other bad news.

3

Practical Skills

BILLING YOUR TIME

Billing is the lifeblood of any law firm. Law firms provide services, for which they bill. If clients pay the bills, and receipts from billing exceed the firm's expenses, the firm is profitable. If bills are not properly sent, or if clients refuse to pay the bills as submitted, the firm's profitability is in jeopardy.

Despite the central place of billing in the economic structure of a law firm, most firms pay scant attention to formal training of junior lawyers in the basic principles of proper billing. For the junior lawyer, forced to learn billing by osmosis, the great likelihood is that mistakes and bad habits will develop, which may cause no small amount of anxiety and even adversely affect a junior lawyer's career development.

Why Billing Matters

Billing matters because it is objective. Every client, to some degree or other, measures the adequacy of legal services by what the services cost, not just in the abstract (hourly rate) but in the aggregate (how much it costs to close a deal or to conclude a litigation).

Senior lawyers, at least to some degree, measure junior lawyers by how many hours they bill, and how efficient they are. All other things being equal, a junior lawyer who bills 20 percent more hours than another junior lawyer is the more valuable. On the other hand, a junior lawyer who can do the same work in 20 percent less time than another junior lawyer is also more valuable because work is being done at a bargain price. No matter how these perhaps contradictory measures are evaluated, the point is that these are objective measures that law firms can and do use to evaluate their junior lawyers.

Within the normal curve of operations, hourly comparisons are mean-
ingless. Two busy junior lawyers who finish the year with a difference
of 10 billable hours between them are, unless some other factors apply,
equally productive.

Yet, it is a mistake to assume that hours do not matter in a law firm,
so long as you are a sufficiently talented lawyer. That may be true in a
small fraction of cases, but for most lawyers, in most firms, hours do
matter.

Pay Attention to the Quota

Most law firms use some official or unofficial quota (or target, or
guideline) for annual hourly billing. You should learn what that number
is and then take steps to meet (or well exceed) it.

The first step is to do some rough calculation of the hours per day
you need to bill in order to meet the quota. Assume (for simplicity) that
the quota is 2,000 hours per year, that you take two weeks off each year
for vacation, and that you usually work 5 days per week. Your daily
target for billing is:

$$2000 \text{ hours/year} \div 50 \text{ weeks/year} \div 5 \text{ days/week} = 8 \text{ hours/day}$$

That number could easily change by changing any of the components:
Raise or lower the annual quota; raise or lower the number of vacation
(and holiday) weeks you take; raise or lower the number of days per
week that you work. Any of those changes will change your daily target.

The next step is to account for any major fluctuations in your daily
hours, which could affect your performance. If you have an extended
slow period, in which you consistently fail to meet your daily billing
target, you may miss the annual quota, even though during some later
period you are busier than normal. The point is that hours lost in one
period must be made up in another.

The final step is to order your lifestyle in a way that makes it possible
to meet (and exceed) your target, within the bounds of how you prefer
to work. Some lawyers are strictly 9-to-5 workers, who work produc-
tively all day and leave. Many others take frequent (unbillable) breaks
throughout the day, and spend a good deal of time at the office after
hours. Some come in very early or stay very late. Others take billable
work home with them and do it in the evenings or on weekends. Try to
find a pattern that makes sense for your personal situation, and stick
with it.

Know the System

Every law firm has some established system for keeping time. Generally, that system is explained in a firm manual or a manual specifically

dedicated to billing practices. The system will likely involve some form of electronic recording of time. Again, there is likely some manual explaining the electronic system. These documents are well worth reviewing.

In addition to these firm-designed billing policies, keep in mind that some clients and matters may require special forms of billing. For example, bankruptcy matters are frequently accounted for with shorter time increments than may be used for other matters. Similarly, some clients (insurance companies, for example) may require special recording of time using unique coding systems that permit easier data retrieval and comparison.

If you have any questions about the billing systems, it is always preferable to ask someone rather than produce a large volume of time records that will require wholesale correction after a mistaken procedure is discovered. Indeed, the discovery of the mistake by a bill-reviewing partner may produce tremendous annoyance, which can be avoided with some basic preventive inquiry.

It is also worth asking questions on some of the more subjective and variable elements of billing. Some firms (and some clients), for example, have strict rules about what constitutes unbillable time (such as travel time, time spent reviewing files, or time spent on establishing general familiarity with a subject matter). Often, however, such rules are not expressly stated, and thus you should ask questions of a supervising lawyer to get directions before billing records are created.

Create a Personal System

Generally, it is preferable to record time as activities occur, to ensure that time records are as accurate as possible. For that purpose, many attorneys use day planners, or daily notepads. Others input their time directly into a computer, or dictate into a recording machine.

Even if it is not possible to record activities precisely as they occur, it is highly desirable to have a regular, daily routine pursuant to which time records are created. Allowing unrecorded time to build up in the course of a busy practice is a bad habit that is too easily established. This bad habit can produce a vast array of adverse consequences: strain on your secretary when you attempt to create a month's worth of time records at the end of a billing period; distraction from your own work when this long-neglected task is finally faced; and the great likelihood that mistakes will be made in the rush to complete records at the last minute.

In that regard, it is important to build into your system an opportunity to review any time records created by your secretary. Just as you would not send out a letter without proofreading it, so too you should not finalize billing records without making sure that they are accurate and professional in appearance. Misspelling your client's name in a billing record, for example, is a surefire way to suggest sloppiness and carelessness—hardly the hallmarks of a competent professional.

Remember that billing records are a form of communication with the client. These records should make it easy for the client to understand what work was done. Entries like "research," or "telephone conference," for example, say nothing about the subject matter or purpose of such activities. Of course, it is also possible to say too much in a billing record. A run-on time entry explaining all of what transpired in a fifteen-minute conversation is an unnecessary waste of time. Find the balance between these extremes by asking yourself how much a client would need to know to have a basic understanding of what you were doing.

Account for All Your Professional Time

In addition to creating records of time spent on billable matters (to be transmitted to clients), your time records should record the remainder of your professional time, including attention to office administration, training, business development, and pro bono work, among others. Law firms typically have systems for recording time in these various categories. Keeping accurate records of nonbillable time will help you to review your own progress. Often, firm administrators are keenly interested in the statistics that may be derived from such records.

Do not attempt to make your own judgments about whether the time you spent on a billable project was really as efficient as it might have been. If you worked for eight hours on a research project, but guess that you might have done the work in four hours, you should not record four hours, without checking with a supervising lawyer. Most law firms have a system to write down or write off inefficient work. Supervising lawyers need to make the judgment about what time should be modified, and should be in a position to tell a client how time records were modified. Your undisclosed writeoff of your time not only cheats you of credit for time actually worked, but prevents the exercise of judgment by a senior lawyer.

If you are concerned that some of your time may have been inefficiently spent, it is appropriate to mention it to a supervising lawyer. That may not be the happiest conversation you will ever have. Yet, supervising lawyers generally understand that junior lawyers (especially lawyers fresh out of law school) may take longer to complete a task than more senior lawyers might take. The choice to use a less-experienced lawyer is theirs, not yours, and the decreased efficiency may be offset by your lower billing rate.

Further, there may be occasion during the course of a project to bring to the attention of a supervising lawyer the fact that the project is taking longer than you originally anticipated. A check-in with the supervising lawyer in that situation can help to reassure you that the senior lawyer really does need to have you continue with the project, even though it may be proceeding more slowly than planned. Checking in, moreover, may also provide an opportunity to get some further advice from the supervising lawyer on how to complete the project more efficiently.

Learning to address billing issues in a forthright manner is part of the process of professional development. As with most things in a law firm, more communication is better than less. Ask questions; develop a system that works for you; and feed back problems to supervising lawyers rather than wait for small problems to become bigger headaches.

WRITING AN OFFICE MEMORANDUM

Sooner or later, in every junior lawyer's first years in a law office, some senior lawyer will ask the junior lawyer to produce an office memorandum. After the panic subsides, the junior lawyer will likely dust off notes from his or her first-year legal writing class, or pull out one or more of the popular legal writing style-books, and begin the painful process of creating his or her first formal work product. The trepidation involved in the experience can be acute, and yet few law firms (and even fewer senior lawyers in such firms) bother to tell junior lawyers exactly what they expect from an office memorandum.

In our highly competitive modern legal world, junior lawyers are rarely assigned to write office memoranda merely to test their mettle. Most often, such memoranda are an important part of the client counseling and advocacy that is the stuff of real lawyering. The experience of drafting office memoranda, moreover, spans the generations from the "old school" to "generation next." Mastering this form is an important step toward developing the skills and recognition from senior lawyers and clients that can lead to a lifetime of success in the law.

This section offers some practical suggestions on how to view the process of preparing an office memorandum. This, of course, is not a comprehensive guide to every situation. Indeed, it is undesirable to view the writing process as a matter of rote. Often, the value of an office memorandum turns as much on its responsiveness to the task at hand as it does on its accuracy, clarity, and thoroughness of research.

Make Sure You Have a Firm Grasp of the Assignment

Before you begin any writing assignment, you do best to ask as many questions as the senior lawyer will tolerate concerning the assignment. The most basic questions include: (1) When is the memorandum due? (2) How long (and how detailed) do you want it to be? (3) What jurisdiction's law applies to the question? (4) What exactly is the issue? (5) What (if any) work product already exists on this subject? These kinds of questions will likely lead to a more general discussion of the background of the client, the problem, and the work that has been done to date related to the problem. The more details you can get about how your work fits in with what has gone on before and what is planned, the easier it will be for you to conceptualize what you are doing and why.

A busy senior lawyer, however, may not have sufficient time to explain all the nuances of the problem. It is up to you to make sure that, in the often brief encounters in which the assignment is communicated, you at least get answers to your most basic questions. If you do not get such answers, or if you do not fully understand the directions you have been given, it is your responsibility to get back to the senior lawyer in a tactful way to ask for further directions. Often, this can be accomplished by providing the senior lawyer with periodic updates on your progress in which you not only state what you have done but solicit feedback on whether you are going about the assignment correctly.

Recognize That One Size Does Not Fit All

When a senior lawyer asks for an office memorandum, he or she may have many different forms in mind. These forms may be arrayed on scales from short, simple, quick, and targeted, to lengthy, complicated, laborious, and sprawling.

Spot Research. Often, a senior lawyer will give you a direction to find a case that stands for a particular proposition. The senior lawyer most likely knows what the law is on the subject and merely wants to confirm (perhaps for a letter to a client or an adversary or for a footnote in a brief) that there is good authority for the proposition. When you get an assignment like that, the senior lawyer may not need an office memorandum at all. Instead, it may be sufficient if you merely find an appropriate case, make a copy of it, and highlight or annotate it in some way to make it easy for the senior lawyer to see the relevant portions of the case.

Nevertheless, a very brief memorandum (perhaps a page or less) may be helpful as a way of summarizing the case and pulling out good language from the opinion. Such a memorandum also has the advantage that it may be preserved for future use in your files and on the firm's word-processing system. Saving a copy of the memorandum will also help if the senior lawyer manages to lose the copy of the case you turn in, and if, months or years from now, you have occasion to revisit the question in another context.

However your work product is preserved, it is important to note that any legal research must be targeted toward finding the best authority on the subject at hand. The definition of "best" may vary with the circumstances, but generally it means both the highest and most recent authority in the relevant jurisdiction. Often, the senior lawyer will want only cases that "come out the right way," in the sense that they not only say what the senior lawyer wants to say, but they also reach the same result as the senior lawyer hopes to obtain in his or her matter.

Because it is often difficult to tell whether a case or other authority is precisely what the senior lawyer wants, it is better to err on the side of producing more than one authority on any given proposition. The senior lawyer may easily review a handful of cases and determine that one of them is the most apt and most persuasive. In the process, the senior lawyer may benefit from reviewing a few other cases that may be less sanguine on the point or that may expose complications that might not otherwise occur to the senior lawyer. In that regard, it is quite appropriate to note potentially adverse portions of any authorities provided to the senior lawyer, and not simply highlight the one or two good sentences from an opinion.

Whatever authorities are provided must be checked to ensure that they remain good law. If there are any questions about subsequent history, they should be noted for the senior lawyer, and copies of any subsequent opinions modifying, questioning, reversing, or overruling an opinion must be provided. It is also good practice to keep careful track (on a notepad, for example) of the paths of legal research that you pursue, so that the senior lawyer may be easily informed of how to retrace those paths, if necessary, or to extend the research to other areas that were not pursued.

The Bullet-Point Memorandum. The senior lawyer may be interested not only in finding some authority for a given proposition, but also in conducting a comprehensive review of all (or all recent) authorities on a given subject. Often, the form of the memorandum is merely a series of blurbs, listing the citation for each case, followed by a very brief description of the case, and one or two relevant quotations from the opinion. Unless the senior lawyer otherwise directs, the cases should be listed in order of persuasive authority (highest court, most recent, most on point first; weak and contrary cases later).

The Full Office Memorandum. These are the memoranda you learned about in law school. Typically, the senior lawyer wants you to consider the facts of a situation and write an analysis of how the relevant law would deal with such facts. The format of such a memorandum is often suggested as including (1) a brief statement of the issue; (2) a concise answer to the question; (3) a brief statement of the relevant rule; (4) analysis of the facts and relevant rule; and (5) a conclusion. That format is not set in stone. Consult with the senior lawyer to determine whether there is a more appropriate or more efficient method of communicating the information that the senior lawyer seeks. Be user-friendly.

Recognize, however, that many senior lawyers will not have any better ideas on how to summarize information than you do. Put yourself in the senior lawyer's place. If you were the senior lawyer, what would you need to know to understand the answer to the legal question posed? Make sure to summarize the facts, as you understand them, as clearly as possible so that the senior lawyer knows whether your conclusion may be affected by an incomplete or incorrect understanding of the situation. Also be especially careful to give a fair explanation of any contrary authority or arguments. The senior lawyer is entitled to know whether his or her position is unshakable or whether it is subject to one or more attacks.

If the memorandum addresses more than one significant issue, take some time to make sure that the sequence and structure of your analysis is easy to follow. For especially lengthy memoranda, consider providing reader aids, like a table of contents and mini-conclusions on each point, before taking up the next point.

The Client Memorandum. This form of memorandum may look nearly the same as any other office memorandum, but often its purpose is different. The client may not want, or need, a balanced treatment of the issue. The memorandum may, for example, be used as the basis for talking points in negotiation with another party. In that event, the client will simply want to know what best arguments can be made in support of its position. Some clients are not interested in lengthy discussion of the fine details of a legal point. The client may simply want to have a very skeletal outline of the issue and an assessment of the likelihood of success. The client memorandum should not be confused with an opinion letter rendered by a law firm in connection with a transaction. The form and purpose of an opinion letter differs substantially from the form and purpose of a legal memorandum to a client. In essence, an opinion letter is not a research memorandum at all (although it may be preceded by such a memorandum). Instead, it is an assurance by a law firm to the participants in a deal that certain corporate regularities have been observed in connection with the deal.

Pure Advocacy. The senior lawyer may also be uninterested in a balanced view of the law on a given point. The senior lawyer may ask you to draft a large or small point for a brief. In some instances, you will be asked to participate fully in the brief-writing exercise where you write one whole argument point heading in the brief, and the senior lawyer writes the other(s). Often, however, the senior lawyer will merely ask you to draft a paragraph or two on a more specific subissue.

A Little Preparation Helps a Lot

Before you begin writing any office memorandum, take some time to gather together everything that you will need to refer to in the memorandum. If there are a few critical cases or authorities, get copies of them and have them ready to review as you work. You will find it frustrating to have to go back to the library (or on-line) to find authorities that you looked at during the course of your research but did not copy or otherwise collect for purposes of writing the memorandum.

Similarly, if there are key documents that may affect your analysis of the facts (a complaint, a contract, a series of letters), make sure that you have copies and have fully reviewed them before you begin writing. There is nothing worse than discovering midway through the writing exercise that your view of the facts is fundamentally wrong. It is also frustrating to stop writing while you try to find key documents for reference in the memorandum. When direct quotation or precise reference to such documents is required, moreover, you will need to have them close at hand.

In addition to asking the senior lawyer precisely what it is that he or she wants in the office memorandum, make sure that you are familiar with the format for office memoranda dictated by your firm. Often, a review of sample office memoranda before you start writing will save a vast amount of editing time. It can also avoid potential embarrassment when the senior lawyer rejects your unique form when you turn the memorandum in.

Pay particular attention to the need to protect client confidentiality. Often, it is appropriate to label an office memorandum as "privileged and confidential." That label may be supplemented with "attorney/client communication" and/or "attorney work product" in appropriate circumstances.

Editing the Memorandum

It is worth discovering the attitude of the senior lawyer toward whether you may provide the memorandum in draft form. In some instances, where the project is collaborative (e.g., you and the senior lawyer are together creating a brief or a memorandum to a client), it may be acceptable to produce an incomplete document, with bracketed sections noting points of fact or law to be filled in by the senior lawyer. Similarly, the senior lawyer may indicate, by restricting the length of the memorandum, that the document is to be only a very brief statement on the issue addressed.

In most instances, however, it is best to assume that the senior lawyer expects a complete, final, and polished piece, which (in theory at least) is suitable for use without any further work by the senior lawyer. That means that the citations provided in the memorandum must be scrupulously accurate and subsequent history correctly noted. Bluebook citation form must be followed, unless otherwise directed by the senior lawyer. It is also important that the memorandum be carefully spell-checked and proofread by human eyes (yours). No word processing program and no midnight-shift proofreader can do the complete job of correcting errors in the memorandum that you can provide.

The point of this obsession with detail is to ensure that, to the extent that you can, you convey the impression that you have taken every step to make sure that the memorandum is a reliable piece of legal research and writing. Obvious mistakes (misspellings, poor grammar, incorrect punctuation) can subtly sabotage your point. The senior lawyer or client must often wonder: If this kind of glaring mistake was made, what other mistakes may have been made in the research and analysis?

CITE-CHECKING

Most junior lawyers, whether involved in litigation or business practice, sooner or later will encounter an assignment to conduct a cite-check of a document. Although law school legal writing courses generally provide a good introduction to cite-checking, the practical problems encountered in a law firm setting require more refined consideration. Cite-checking may not be the most glamorous part of being a lawyer. Yet, it is an essential skill, which leads to more complicated work. Junior lawyers who master this essential skill can differentiate themselves from other junior lawyers who may feel that the work is boring or beneath them. By mastering the details of the profession, a junior lawyer can help serve the client and help demonstrate qualifications for the bigger things to come. This section aims to provide a short list of practical questions and answers to guide junior lawyers who take up their first cite-checking tasks.

What Is the Point of This Task?

In general, legal memoranda, whether they are filed in court or merely circulated as office memoranda among lawyers and their clients, are designed to inform (and often persuade) their audience. The point of including citations to legal authorities is to demonstrate that the propositions of law are well-considered and supported and to permit the reader to review those authorities easily so that the reader can make an informed decision.

In that vein, the accuracy of legal citations may be critical. A missed citation (reversal of a decision, for example) can be devastating. A court or a client could not help but lose confidence in a lawyer or law firm responsible for such a mistake. On a less dramatic note, however, scrupulous accuracy of legal citations subtly enhances the message of any legal memorandum, which should be, "You can rely on this document to give complete and accurate information."

For the junior lawyer there is yet another agenda. Cite-checking is one of the building blocks of legal experience. In their early years, junior lawyers learn to research, cite-check, and write legal memoranda. As junior lawyers gain experience in these areas, and as they demonstrate their growing competence, senior lawyers may begin to entrust them with more complicated and more substantial tasks. A junior lawyer who sweats the details on mundane, relatively minor, tasks like cite-checking shows tenacity, teamwork, and professionalism that is often a ticket to greater things.

How Much Work Should Be Done?

Like many things in law, there is no "one size fits all" version of cite-checking. The assigning lawyer may merely wish to check cited authorities to make sure that there is no adverse subsequent history. But there could be more: checking all the quotes to make sure that they are accurate; checking the particular pages cited; conforming citations to Blue Book form. The assigning lawyer might also want the junior lawyer to read the memorandum for content and to fix grammar, usage, spelling, and punctuation errors. The amount of work expected will often depend on how much time there is to complete the memorandum and how much the supervising lawyer has already polished the document. The junior lawyer cannot know, without asking, precisely what the senior lawyer has in mind.

More to the point, it will be too late if, after completing the task, the junior lawyer learns that he or she has seriously misunderstood how much work the senior lawyer expected would be devoted to the task. If the senior lawyer expected a top-to-bottom review, and the junior lawyer has merely checked the basics, failure to do more may give the appearance of laziness or irresponsibility. Indeed, if the senior lawyer expects a complete review, and does not learn until the last minute that this work has not been done, the project itself may be in jeopardy. Conversely, if the senior lawyer merely expects a "once over" of the document, and the junior lawyer spends hours on the project, the time spent might have to be written off, at great annoyance.

Most effective senior lawyers know how to give specific directions on this kind of task. If such directions are not given, however, the junior lawyer must ask before beginning the work. A junior lawyer might give the senior lawyer a checklist of the work planned. The junior lawyer might also begin the task and report in periodically on progress so that the senior lawyer can tell whether more work should be added to the project. If the junior lawyer is at all uncertain about doing too much or too little, he or she must take the time to get these directions straight.

Even if the senior lawyer does not ask for it, however, the junior lawyer should generally not hesitate to call attention to any glaring errors that may be discovered. Despite word-processing gadgets like spell-checkers, errors can arise in long and complicated legal documents, which overworked attorneys can simply miss. Making the extra effort to spot such errors will almost always be well received.

How Should the Work Be Recorded?

There are two major considerations here. The first has to do with the junior lawyer's own records of progress in the work. The junior lawyer should have a system that makes it possible to capture the information accurately as it is gathered, even if that information does not always make its way into a revised version of the document. Many attorneys make a copy of the document that is to be checked and make notations on the copy (check marks, or other notes); others use a separate legal pad. Whatever the system, the junior attorney needs to keep track of the citations that have been checked.

The junior attorney should generally note: (1) Has the case been Shepardized? (2) Has Blue Book form been checked? (3) Have quotes on page references been verified? (4) Has subsequent history been checked? Each of these steps should be done separately so that the document is checked several times for different potential problems. Absent some form of checklist, it is possible to miss one of these steps with a citation and thus fail to catch an error.

The other issue that must be considered is how to communicate the proposed changes to the supervising attorney. Generally, absent specific direction from a supervising attorney, it is best not to make changes directly in the electronic word processing version of the document. It is much better to bring proposed changes to the attention of the supervising lawyer before the changes are made. The great likelihood is that the supervising attorney will not want to make all the suggested changes. If the supervising lawyer has to "back out" changes made in the electronic word processing version of the document, inefficiency and annoyance may result. Thus, at a minimum, changes in the electronic word processing version of the document should never be made without the express approval of the supervising lawyer.

A marked draft of the document, showing proposed changes to citations, may be the best way to communicate corrections. If the supervising attorney approves of the proposed changes, the marked draft can be given to a word processing operator to fix the document. If the supervising attorney has additional changes or wishes to reject some portions of the proposed changes, it is also easy to mark the draft for word processing.

What Parts of Subsequent History Are Important?

In general, there are two kinds of citations: those that are helpful to a client's position, and those that are harmful. Although, as a matter of ethics, all relevant subsequent history generally must be disclosed, the question of what is relevant may depend on whether a citation is helpful or harmful.

If a citation is helpful, it may be quite important to show that the authority remains good law or that it has been extended. For example, suppose that there is a federal district court opinion granting a motion to dismiss on a legal ground that is helpful to the case at hand. It may be useful to note that reconsideration of that opinion was denied by the district court, that the decision was affirmed by the appellate court (and *en banc* review denied), and that certiorari was denied by the Supreme Court. It might also be worthwhile noting whether other courts have cited the opinion on the pertinent point. If, on the other hand, the citation is unhelpful, there may be no particular need to enhance the value of the citation by showing that reconsideration was denied; that after the decision was affirmed, *en banc* review was denied; or that the opinion has been cited with approval in other jurisdictions. It might, however, be helpful to show that other courts have questioned the reasoning in the opinion or refused to extend it to facts beyond those in the original opinion.

Again, there are ethics rules on disclosure of relevant history. The point here, however, is that even such things as citation form can be affected by a desire to persuade. Thus, within the bounds of ethics, the extent of disclosure of subsequent history may depend on whether a citation helps or hurts a client's position.

When in doubt, of course, it is preferable to err on the side of suggesting too much subsequent history. The supervising attorney can always choose to trim back subsequent history citations that are not considered relevant. If the supervising attorney is not given a complete recitation of subsequent history, however, some relevant history may be missed. For that reason, many junior attorneys print out complete subsequent history pages from electronic services, which they offer to the supervising attorney or at least point to in asking the supervising attorney about any subsequent history issues for which the answer (on how much history to include) was not immediately apparent.

Where subsequent history is not self-explanatory, it may be extremely helpful to the supervising lawyer to have a copy of the opinion embodying the subsequent history. For example, if a trial court decision has been modified on appeal, it will not be possible for the supervising attorney to decide whether the trial court decision is still good law without reading the decision from the appellate court. Similarly, one must read the appellate court decision before indicating in the subsequent history citation that an opinion has been reversed or modified on grounds other than the point for which the case is being cited. For that reason, if there is any doubt about the significance of subsequent history, it often is preferable to provide the supervising lawyer with copies of the opinions that constitute subsequent history.

Is the Blue Book the Only Reference for Citation Form?

Law school experience often conditions junior lawyers to rely upon the Blue Book as the only reference source for information on proper citation form. There are, however, several additional factors that may affect citation form. First, local rules of court or rules for the individual judge may require special citation forms. The junior lawyer should try to become familiar with such peculiar rules. Where litigation is being conducted in an unfamiliar jurisdiction, the junior lawyer should make sure to obtain copies of such rules rather than assume that the supervising lawyer will obtain them.

Second, there may be abbreviations, proper names, or other citation forms that have been consistently used in other papers affecting the client or this project. The junior lawyer should try to become familiar with such forms, either by obtaining precedent papers or by asking the supervising lawyer whether there are any conventions that have been used in connection with this project.

Finally, at a minimum, the junior lawyer should be prepared for the possibility that a supervising lawyer may have personal preferences about citation forms that are not entirely consistent with the Blue Book. Although the Blue Book is the starting point for citation form checking, the junior lawyer should not insist that a document strictly comply with the Blue Book if the supervising lawyer prefers otherwise. The junior lawyer's role is to suggest proposed changes; the supervising lawyer's role is to exercise judgment in implementing the best of the proposed changes.

Are Electronic Databases Acceptable for Cite-Checking?

Although many senior lawyers were raised in an era when computers were not ubiquitous, and citations had to be checked exclusively by paper records, today's junior lawyers are increasingly skilled in using electronic research formats. Indeed, some law firms have done away entirely with paper volumes (like Shepard's) and essentially rely on electronic research to perform cite-checking functions. In general, electronic research is a perfectly acceptable method of cite-checking, with a few caveats.

First, electronic databases are only as good as the information they contain. If an electronic database is not frequently updated to reflect up-to-the-minute information (like the filing of a petition for certiorari or the issuance of an unpublished opinion), it is possible that the cite-check will miss important information.

Second, the editorial assistance provided by an electronic research service is not necessarily geared to the need of one's own specific case. For example, the West KeyCite system uses red and yellow status flags to warn of negative case histories. These flags can help alert the junior lawyer to the need to check this history. The junior lawyer should not, however, abandon judgment in response to such editorial notes. The subsequent history should be reviewed in its complete text form before any decisions are made on whether to keep the citation in the document and on how to refer to any negative subsequent history.

Electronic research may suggest avenues of argument that might not have been apparent when a document was first drafted. For example, the West KeyCite system has the ability to check an opinion for negative treatment of the authorities cited in it (which could suggest that the opinion was not well-reasoned). With the immense power of computing, legal research can be extended to a virtually indefinite point. Thus, before using electronic research to perform cite-checking, it is very important to confirm a specific plan for that research. Is the research solely to check obvious subsequent history, or is it intended as a "no stone unturned" project? Before the expense and time are incurred, the junior lawyer should make certain of the directions for the electronic research project.

Keep in mind that certain citations (like statutes, regulations, and agency decisions) may not be easily checked with automated citation services. For these, it is very important to make certain what information the electronic service will retrieve and what it may omit. Often, for such things as legislative history, it will be necessary to revert to the paper records. Electronic research may help guide, but will not necessarily substitute for, that work.

What Are the Final Steps in Cite-Checking?

High-quality legal documents often go through several drafts. For the junior lawyer, the job of cite-checking may require checking the same document more than once. As changes are made (citations added or deleted, subsequent history noted, and new points made), the document must be reviewed again. Keeping a record of the citation information that has been previously gathered will aid immeasurably in this process. The junior lawyer can boost efficiency by quickly checking citations that have been previously verified and concentrating on any new citations, or changes in citations, that have been made in subsequent drafts of the document.

Typically, each new draft of the document will be marked "draft," with the specific date and time of the draft noted so that it is possible for all who review the document to make sure that they are examining the most recent version of the document. The junior lawyer should make sure that the draft of the document being reviewed is the most recent version so that the cite-checking is performed most effectively and changes can be most effectively communicated to the supervising lawyer and word processing operator.

The final portion of the work often will be creation of any reader's aids, such as tables of contents and authorities. There are word processing programs that will automatically create these tables, but these programs are only as good as the information in the original document. Thus, it is generally best to put the document (including citations) into final form and then extract the headings and citations for purposes of creation of tables.

The citations in the tables should not require checking for subsequent history, which should be completed by the time the text of the document is finalized. A final check on citations in the tables for such mundane things as citation form, spelling of case names, and punctuation, however, may be a useful way to catch errors that may not be as easily apparent in the text. Any changes made in the citations in the tables must also be made in the text.

EDITING

For many new lawyers just starting in practice, the transition from the isolated work of a law student to the teamwork of a law firm can be jarring. Even such basic tasks as editing a legal document may seem daunting when it is unclear what the senior lawyer expects or how the adequacy of the editing work will be judged. This section highlights some important factors to keep in mind when approaching an editing assignment.

How Much Time Is Available?

Editing, like most legal writing tasks (research, cite-checking, etc.) is a potentially never-ending task. Given unlimited time, virtually every legal document can be improved in some way. Yet, there never is unlimited time. The letter must be sent; the contract draft must be exchanged; the brief must be filed. Beyond the basic pressure to complete the task on time, most clients will question the expense of a seemingly endless process of editing. A point must always come at which a lawyer says, "This is as good a document as I have time to make it."

If you are editing your own work, the task of watching the clock may be relatively simple. You must set aside enough time in the writing process to review your work before it goes out the door. For simple documents (like e-mail and basic letters), this may be no more than a "once over" review to check names, dates, spelling, and typos. For larger documents, especially those that are subject to review and input from the client, senior lawyers, and co-counsel, it may be critical to include sufficient time in the writing process to permit everyone to comment and time for all such comments to be integrated into the document and reviewed again.

What Is Your Principal Purpose?

Related to the question of the time available for the editing task is the question of what principal purposes the editing task may serve. Although it is often possible to combine many tasks in a single editing exercise, it is helpful to conceive of the editing process on an escalating scale, from the most basic to the higher order functions. Depending on many factors (time, your seniority, and the degree to which the document has already been edited, among others), your editing work may fall at one end or the other of this spectrum. If you are unclear which of the following functions you should be performing, you must inquire.

- Proofreading: Often, lawyers who have spent a great deal of time working on a document grow tired of reviewing and revising the document. A pair of fresh eyes can often spot errors, inconsistencies, and unclear passages. Thus, although the proofreading function is basic, it can be quite valuable.

- Editing for Content: The editor in this role generally seeks to make a document clearer, more accurate, shorter, simpler, easier to follow, more consistent with other relevant documents, and (in the case of litigation-related documents) more persuasive. This kind of editing work can be quite time-consuming and requires good editing skills and judgment.
- Editing for Concepts: The editor involved in this kind of "big picture" review looks to see whether a document contains reference to all the necessary concepts so that the reader can understand the deal or be persuaded by the client's position in litigation. The editor may also suggest reordering or striking references to some concepts that may appear to be redundant, unnecessary, and unhelpful. This kind of editing may involve less time but generally requires a high degree of familiarity and facility with the problem addressed by the document.

Who Controls the Document?

The essential dynamic of the editing process is communication. Someone creates a document, and then someone suggests changes to be made in the document. Where you control the document, and no one else needs to review it, the communication may be entirely with yourself. You draft the document, print it out, make notes on changes, then make changes in the document.

More likely, however, there will be at least one other person involved in the editing process. That person may be your secretary or a word-processing operator, who may input the changes you note on the draft of the document. Quite often, there may be several people who suggest changes in a document. There are several points to keep in mind whenever more than one person is involved in the editing process. If you are unsure about any of these points, you must inquire.

- There should be only one person in control of the document (the principal editor). The principal editor should be responsible for receiving and integrating comments, producing each new draft, and distributing the drafts to all reviewers.
- There should be only one working version of the document, which all reviewers are reviewing at any given time. It is often more difficult to integrate two versions of the same document than it is to take multiple comments on the same working document from separate sources. Part of the responsibility of the principal editor is to make sure that all editors are looking at the same version of the document. For this reason, it is common to include a date and

time indicator on each draft of a document, or otherwise note the generation of the document ("first draft," "second draft," etc.).

- There should be some agreement on the method by which comments are provided. Most commonly, "hard" copies of the working document are returned to the principal editor (often with courtesy copies to all other editors), with comments handwritten on the draft. Longer comments may be typed as proposed inserts to the document. Other methods of editing are possible. For example, the document may be passed in electronic form from one editor to another, with each editor making changes and passing them on (often with "blacklining") to show the proposed changes). The point is that the editors need to know how comments will be shared before they begin the process of altering the document. Again, if you are unclear about the process, you must inquire before making changes in the document.

Some Do's and Don'ts in the Editing Process

Many of the following pointers may seem simple and self-evident, but you must pay close attention to them.

- Make sure that you have all the information you need before you start the editing process. In addition to getting answers to the questions outlined earlier, make sure that you have a complete copy of the most recent version of the document to be edited, that you have copies of any materials referenced in the document, and that you have any table of contents or other reader's aid that is meant to accompany the document.
- Read everything. Do not presume that the author has already fixed the minutiae of the document (dates, headers, "re" line, caption, title, point headings, closing, etc.). Everything means everything.
- Give yourself enough room to write out your comments. If the document is single-spaced and may require extensive comments, consider photo-reducing it to give you larger margins for comments, or print it out in double-spaced form. Alternatively, conduct one edit to address "big picture" issues and another to fix more mundane problems. Returning a document with cramped, hard-to-follow editorial comments often creates more problems, as an author or word-processing operator struggles to follow your suggestions.
- Learn and consistently use standard editorial symbols. Pay attention to repeated instances where your editorial marks are misunderstood by your secretary or word processing staff. Consistent

errors suggest that you need to take steps to communicate your editorial changes more clearly.

- Don't simply ask questions on a document. A question like "Could this be shorter," is much less helpful than suggestions as to specific cuts. Be sensitive, moreover, to the fact that some authors are particularly anxious about criticism of their work. For them especially, showing what you think may be clearer, shorter, or more persuasive writing is much less threatening than asking questions that may seem challenging.
- Don't fix it, if it ain't broke. There are many styles of writing. If your suggestions are more stylistic than substantive, resist the temptation to edit for editing's sake alone.
- Don't forget to check the changes. Often, editorial suggestions are misinterpreted or misapplied. In many instances, moreover, the physical process of editing a document introduces new errors (typos, formatting, pagination, etc.). Part of the editing task is to check to make sure that editorial changes have been properly implemented.

MEETING MANAGEMENT

Meetings, large and small, formal and informal, are a regular part of most lawyers' professional experience. Yet, law school does little (if anything) to prepare new lawyers for their participation in meetings, and most law firms offer little (if any) practical training regarding meeting management.

This section aims to provide some practical pointers on meetings, focusing especially on the role of the junior lawyer. The focus here will be on larger, more formal meetings. Many of the suggestions may also apply to smaller, more impromptu meetings, but generally the success of such meetings is less critical, largely because there are greater opportunities to conduct follow-up meetings, or other communications, to complete the tasks touched upon in an informal meeting.

Establishing the Meeting's Purpose

The first question to address before arranging any meeting is whether there is any need for a meeting at all. Some meetings (periodic committee meetings, for example) are required. Most others, however, are convened for one or more specific purposes. If it is possible to accomplish such purposes without meeting, often the most efficient course is to avoid meeting. In addition, with modern technology, it may be possible to conduct a meeting other than face-to-face. Telephone conferences, video connections, and instant messaging exchanges (to name only a few) are all available as alternatives.

From the junior lawyer's perspective, in many instances you will not be responsible for convening a meeting or establishing its purpose. Nevertheless, it is important for you to understand the purpose(s) of any meetings in which you became involved. Your ability to assist other participants in the meeting depends on your understanding of the focus of the meeting and the elements necessary to ensure that the meeting is a success. You should, therefore, ask questions of the senior lawyers involved in the meeting to help you understand the purposes and priorities of the meeting.

Logistical Preparation

Once a decision has been made to meet, and the general purpose(s) of the meeting have been established, there will quickly follow a series of logistical questions concerning the meeting. As a junior lawyer, you may be asked to help resolve one or more of these issues. At a minimum, you should be aware of the developing answers to these questions and should offer your assistance to the senior lawyers involved in the meeting to help ensure that these logistical issues are addressed.

- Who is invited to the meeting? Some participants may be essential to the meeting; ensuring their availability may be a critical first task in setting up the meeting. Other participants may be required for only a portion of the meeting, or their information may be transmitted in a form other than a verbal report at the meeting. Some potential participants may be excluded to keep the size of the meeting manageable or because their participation is not really essential. Decisions about which potential participants to invite to the meeting must be made early, and follow-up steps (confirmation of the schedule and reminder notices) will be required to make the meeting successful.
- When will the meeting take place? In addition to making sure that the calendar date is available for all the participants, it will be important to consider how much time is required for the meeting. Setting a specific time limit for the meeting can help to improve efficiency (forcing the participants to focus on critical issues). Too little time, however, may mean that some agenda items must be ignored or that the meeting will conclude without accomplishing its essential purpose.
- Where will the meeting take place? Some decisions on meeting place may be dictated by convenience. There may, for example, be a central location that is convenient to most participants. Other

decisions may be affected by strategy or politics. In conducting a negotiation, for example, it may be preferable to hold meetings on one's home turf; in conducting a pitch for new business to a client, it may be essential to go to the client's location. In other instances, a neutral, off-site meeting location may be preferred.

- What facilities are required? The size of the meeting room is just one of the many questions that may arise. There may be a need to make travel and hotel arrangements for some of the participants. There will likely be a requirement for refreshments (and perhaps full meals) during the meeting. There may be needs for photocopying, audiovisual, word processing, and other services to support the meeting process. For some meetings, translators may be necessary. All these details (and more) must be considered, and arranged, in advance of the meeting.

Setting the Agenda

Well-run meetings generally have an agenda. Drafting the agenda, circulating it for comments, and finalizing the agenda in advance of the meeting—any or all of these tasks may fall to you as the junior lawyer preparing for a meeting.

The agenda should be short, simple, and clear. The most important items should generally be listed first. It may be worthwhile to indicate the main purpose(s) of the meeting. It may also be worthwhile to list specific times for discussion of agenda items (thus indicating the priority of the items).

Once an agenda is drafted, it is important to circulate the agenda to participants for their comments. Circulation of the agenda can help spark preparation for the meeting by the participants. Feedback on the agenda, moreover, may shape your views on logistical aspects of the meeting (whether, for example, the meeting time can be shortened because not all agenda items need to be addressed at the meeting, or whether the time must be lengthened because there is an additional important issue to be discussed). If any changes are made in the agenda, be sure to recirculate the revised agenda before the meeting.

Roles at the Meeting

Your junior status may confine the scope of your participation in meetings, at least at the outset of your career. Nevertheless, you can contribute (in small, and eventually large ways) to the success of a meeting. Keen observation of the participants in a meeting, and the roles they play, moreover, will improve your understanding and enhance your ability to contribute to future meetings. Meeting roles may include the following:

- Supporter: The supporter's function is to make sure that the meeting runs smoothly. You should check the meeting location the day of the meeting to make sure the room is ready: seats arranged, lighting sufficient, audiovisual equipment in place, refreshments ordered, acoustics satisfactory (and anything else that may affect the convenience and comfort of the participants). During the meeting, even if you are not in the meeting room, you should remain available at all times. You may also need to enlist additional supporters and staff to assist with the meeting.
- Presenter: You may be asked to give (or to assist in giving) a presentation at the meeting. Often, the presentation may be nothing more than a brief oral report. At other times, much greater detail and perhaps a written report will be required. It is critical to know how much time is allotted to your presentation and to know the expectations of the meeting participants regarding the level of detail and focus of your presentation. Hand-outs, audiovisual displays, and assignments for discussion (if there will be more than one presenter)—all must be worked out in advance. Your goal, in most instances, will be to get to the point quickly, while making sure that all participants fully understand what you have to say.
- Secretary: Most formal meetings have a secretary, whose function is to take notes and to prepare minutes of the meeting. The secretary often does not participate directly in the meeting, in order to focus on preparing complete and accurate notes. Minutes of the meeting should be drafted as soon as possible after the meeting concludes. Minutes should be short, clear, and unbiased. Assignments (if any) should be noted, as should any deadlines. Prompt circulation of draft minutes will encourage prompt action on any issues raised. Generally, the form of minutes should be reviewed by senior lawyers before circulation to any wider group of meeting participants. Any issues of privilege attendant to the meeting and the minutes should be discussed in advance to ensure that privilege is preserved where possible.
- Chair: The function of the chair is to guide the discussion at a meeting, ensuring that any discussion is relevant to the agenda, that all participants have a fair opportunity to express their views, that disruptions are minimized, that the group moves through the agenda points with reasonable dispatch, and that the group reaches decision (where necessary) on any critical points. In most instances, only a fairly senior person will be asked to chair a meeting, but there will be occasions (soon) when you are among the most senior participants in a meeting or when you will be asked to substitute for a senior person who suddenly becomes unavailable to serve as chair. Your confidence in your ability to perform

as chair will depend largely on your preparation for the meeting. The more you consider, in advance, the issues likely to arise at the meeting and the interests of the participants in the meeting, the more likely that you will be able to control the meeting in an efficient and effective way.

Informal/Smaller Meetings

Virtually all of the structure and dynamics of a large, formal meeting may be reflected in smaller, more informal meetings. Such meetings may range from chance encounters with other lawyers in a hallway at your law firm to impromptu internal team meetings, to "meet and greet" sessions with clients and prospective clients. In all such settings (and especially in larger, more formal meetings) you should constantly ask the following questions:

- What is the point of this meeting? If you are unsure, ask (before, during, or after the meeting). If you do not know the purpose, it will be difficult to contribute to the outcome.
- What is your role? If you have no role, you may not belong at the meeting. If you have a role, you should recognize it (and perhaps state what you think that role is to the other participants in the meeting).
- Are you contributing to the meeting? Your contribution may include handling the logistics of the meeting. It may also include presenting information and sharing your opinions. But there is also contribution in listening to the views of others and in supporting others who wish to express themselves. It should be a rare meeting when you either do 100 percent of the talking or 100 percent of the listening.
- Are you taking responsibility? Effective meetings depend on participants who are prepared for discussion and who are willing to accept the assignments that may come from such discussion. The "duck and cover" approach to the work of a meeting encourages other participants to shirk responsibility. Show leadership by taking responsibility.
- Even the most junior lawyer can contribute to an effective meeting. Recognition by your peers and supervisors as an effective meeting participant will enhance your status and reputation and will ultimately contribute to your success in whatever field you may choose.

CONFERENCE CALLS

Sooner or later as a lawyer, you will participate in your first conference call. Eventually, conference calls may become a regular part of your professional life. This section aims to provide some insight into the practical elements of arranging and conducting a conference call. The section approaches such calls from the perspective of a junior lawyer who wishes to know what role he or she should play in the conference call process.

Begin with the recognition that a conference call is essentially a meeting, conducted by telephone. The most basic preparation for a conference call is the same as for any meeting. You need to know when and how the call will take place. What is the precise time of the call? If the time of the call is figured from a time zone other than your own, what will be the time of the call where you are? Is there a dial-in-number, or will the host of the call arrange to call you? Is there an identification code you need to know to gain access to the call? If there are problems gaining access, whom should you call?

Make sure you have answers to these kinds of questions well in advance of the call. If you (or a more senior lawyer in your firm) are hosting the call, make sure that this kind of information is distributed to participants well in advance. Consider also, as host, taking some steps, shortly before the call, to remind participants of the call, the time, and the procedure for participating in the call.

Consider also the means by which you plan to participate in the call. If you are out of your office at the time of the call, for example, you may need to ensure that there is a land line available for you to participate in the call. Use of a cellular telephone may disrupt your participation in the call (to the annoyance of others on the call). Static from cellular telephone use (or background noise from the use of a public telephone) may also annoy others on the call. Finally, although hardly least important, use of a cellular telephone may jeopardize privacy and risk waiver of privilege for the call (at least in some jurisdictions).

As with any other meeting, your preparation for a conference call should include inquiry as to whether an agenda exists for the call and whether any particular documents will be discussed on the call. Unlike face-to-face meetings, it may be difficult to distribute agendas and documents at the time of the call. Thus, you should gather such materials in advance. (Similarly, if you are hosting the call, you should make sure that the materials are distributed in advance.)

Pay particular attention to the agenda. Often, as a junior lawyer, you will have great difficulty interrupting a conference call to add a point for discussion not set out on the agenda. It is often easier to consult with the host of the call in advance to add items to the agenda than it is to add points during the call. At very least, if you have a point to add to the agenda, do so at the beginning of the call rather than jump in with it at the end when participants may be eager to end the call. Often, at the outset of a call, the host will review the agenda. This may be the occasion for you to add your point to the list of items to be discussed.

Preparation is also key in dealing with clients and senior lawyers in your firm. Where others on your team (client representatives and colleagues in your firm) are not at the same location at the time of the call, it may be difficult to consult privately with them during the call. You may thus be required either to hold back in the discussion (for lack of authority from your team) or advance what may be ill-advised points, which consultation in advance would have revealed. If you have discussed your points in advance with your team, you will generally feel more comfortable participating in the call.

Protocol during the call is also important. At the outset of the call, participants typically announce themselves and their affiliations. The host may also check off a roster of participants. It is generally quite bad form to lurk on a call, never announcing your participation (or, perhaps worse, leaping into the discussion unannounced after the call begins). Where there are many participants on a call and they do not all know each other's voices, participants may often identify themselves again during the call as a preface to any remarks.

Although participants will often use speakerphones (especially for long conference calls and those where there is a group of participants at one location), caution and courtesy are in order. A speakerphone may pick up unwanted comments (including privileged side conversations and offensive joking remarks). A speakerphone may also pick up extraneous noise (typing, shuffling papers, the sounds of eating or drinking). Whatever you would not do in a face-to-face meeting, you should not do on a conference call. The fact that participants cannot see you does not mean that they cannot hear you (and think less of you as a result). At very least, use the mute button if you are engaged in noisy activities during the call. So, too, if by shouting into the speakerphone you may annoy other call participants, you should also pick up the telephone.

Caution and courtesy also apply at the end of a conference call. If you know in advance that your time is constrained, you should not wait until the end of your time (with many points left to cover on the agenda) to announce that you have no more time for the call. Worse yet, of course, you should not simply drop off the call unannounced, leaving others on the call to wonder where (and when) you have gone.

Similarly, during the call, if you must take a break from the call for some reason, you should let the other participants know that you will be off-line, and announce your return when it occurs. Make sure that if you place the conference call on hold, you are not consigning the other participants to listen to annoying music while they wait for your return.

Before the call ends in its entirety, moreover, there may be several ministerial points to cover (as there would be at any other meeting). Do the participants plan to speak again (and, if so, when)? Is there any list of "to do" items generated from the call? (Reviewing such a list at the end of the call may help to crystallize the results the discussion had during the earlier parts of the call). Will notes of the call be prepared (and who will prepare the notes)? These are among the points that may be discussed before the call ends. Thus, do not exit the call until you are sure that it is really over.

If the call (or at least your portion of it) is over, hang up. On occasion, a call may continue with a reduced roster of participants. It is extremely bad form (and perhaps unethical) to linger on a call unannounced after other participants believe you have dropped off. If you need to speak to one of the participants, call him or her separately after you are off the call.

The foregoing bits of advice about conference calls say nothing about the substance of what may occur on such calls. It is not possible to prepare for all the styles of communication you may encounter in such calls. There are, however, a few aspects of the telephone medium to consider.

- The mind often wanders during conference calls, especially calls with many participants where most people are not speaking. If you wish to ensure that your point is heard, understood, and remembered, make sure that it is stated simply and clearly. Often, repetition of a key point or key phrase will help ensure that every participant gets it.
- Long conference calls, especially those without an agenda, can devolve into disorder as time progresses. Any key point is thus often best stated at the outset of the call (and/or repeated during the crystallization time at the end of the call).
- The telephone does not permit visual cues. Points of emphasis, for example, must come from auditory cues such as repetition, slowed pace for key items, or a simple statement like "This is important." Jokes and banter, to the extent that they require visual cues to maintain good feeling, should be avoided. The give-and-take of conversation, moreover, is not modulated by visual cues on a call. It is thus important for each conference call participant to be patient and wait his or her turn to speak so that participants do not end up drowning each other out.

In the arena of the conference call, planning and preparation are more important than volume, speed, or aggressiveness. The successful conference call participant speaks his or her piece carefully and courteously and allows others to do the same.

PUBLIC SPEAKING

For many new associates, just entering a law firm, the sum of their public speaking experience may consist of one moot court round in law school. There is a sense, moreover, that success in a law firm (at least for those who do not intend to become litigators) has nothing to do with public speaking ability. Even future litigators may assume that because their chances of seeing the inside of a courtroom soon seem so slim, development of public speaking skills and experience can be deferred to a later point in a career.

Those views are shortsighted. No matter what the career path, and no matter what the speed of one's own progress, the ability to compose and deliver clear, effective oral communication will have a significant effect on a junior lawyer's success, starting from the very outset of a professional career. This section aims to highlight the ways in which public speaking can be important and to suggest ways by which speaking ability and experience can be developed.

Begin with the recognition that most senior lawyers (and most clients) can at times be extremely busy. By contrast to law school (and even the summer associate experience) where most projects have a long lead time, soon after a junior lawyer starts at a law firm, there will be the first of many occasions when a senior lawyer or client will ask for quickie advice on some subject. In this situation, there will be no time for contemplative research and writing. If you are lucky, you might get a very brief period to collect your thoughts and be prepared to answer questions. But your advice must be oral, and it must be immediate.

The keys to communicating effectively in this situation are really the keys to effective oral communication in general.

- Answer the question. Although the explanation and background for an answer may be very important, senior lawyers and clients generally start with a fairly specific question (or set of questions) to which they would like an answer. Just as you would compose a question for purposes of an office memorandum, oral advice should generally begin with a statement of the question and the short answer. The answer, in some instances, may not be definitive ("I have not been able to find dispositive law on this point" or "I need to do additional research to answer this question"). But the listener should at least know what you thought the question was and what conclusion you have reached in the time allotted.

- Outline your reasoning. Be prepared for the possibility that your listener will not give you a lot of time to explain yourself. Thus, even if you have much more to say, develop an outline of just the two or three major points in support of your conclusion, which you should be able to deliver in a minute or less. You may also want to develop a more detailed version of the outline, from which you would be prepared to provide a more complete explanation, if given the chance. This more detailed outline may also be helpful when questions come from your listener.
- Speak with confidence about what you know. In asking for quick advice on a subject, senior lawyers and clients are generally looking to make a judgment about whether a decision can be taken on limited information or whether more full-scale research and analysis must be done. If you are certain that you have the essential answer to a question, but you express the conclusion so tentatively that it appears that you are unsure, then the listener may conclude that your research and analysis are incomplete.
- Do not think that this situation is unique. Throughout your career you will be called by senior lawyers and clients who want to check out an issue. These situations are the essence of the attorney/client advice paradigm. Mastering the ability to give oral advice in this situation is thus critical to becoming a fully-functioning lawyer.

There will soon come, moreover, a host of other situations where your oral communication abilities will be tested. Junior corporate lawyers, for example, may participate in negotiating sessions with other counsel and parties, where public speaking may be required. Junior litigators may similarly find themselves involved in settlement negotiations, and eventually in court conferences and other proceedings. Many junior lawyers, moreover, participate in the firm's recruiting and client development activities, all of which depend, at least to some degree, on good oral communication skills.

How, then, to gain the experience necessary to become comfortable in the many public speaking situations you may encounter? The following are a few possibilities:

- Some firms have internal public speaking training programs. These programs are often geared to the special needs and interests of lawyers and may focus in particular on the problems encountered by novice public speakers.
- Many firms have outlets for other internal public speaking opportunities, such as monthly group luncheons, at which subjects of general interest are addressed. Your firm may also have formal training programs, in which you may be able to participate as an instructor.

- Bar associations and continuing legal education groups often look for speakers, especially in hot or developing areas. Your firm's business development coordinator may be able to assist in getting assignments to speak to such groups. More generally, schools at every level (secondary, college, law school) may accept speakers and teachers (especially on a volunteer basis).
- Civic, political, and religious groups (especially those with which you already have an affiliation) may be interested in discussion of legal topics and other subjects that affect businesspeople and community leaders.

Even a brief, limited speaking experience can be valuable. The process of developing a topic, outlining it, and practicing and presenting a speech in a conversational manner will enhance your self-confidence and ease your preparation for the public speaking opportunities you will encounter in your professional capacity. Ultimately, the self-assurance that you can speak effectively will serve you well in all aspects of your career, from private client counseling sessions to the largest public gatherings.

4

Substantive Skills

WHAT LAW SCHOOL DIDN'T TEACH YOU
ABOUT BUSINESS PRACTICE

Law school, in theory, should be capable of preparing you for a career as a business practice lawyer. There are many courses that are relevant to business practice: corporations, securities regulations, and corporate finance (to name only a few). Yet, law school has a particularly difficult time imparting much information about the practical aspects of business practice. Studying cases may help you to understand such basic concepts as the fiduciary duties of corporate officers and directors, but the study of cases will not be of much help in negotiating and closing a deal (and the many other practical tasks that business practice lawyers must be able to perform).

This section aims to outline some of the most important lessons that junior business practice lawyers must learn in the first few years of practice. This list, by necessity, is incomplete, as the experience and focus of each junior business lawyer will differ and may easily extend to important subjects not discussed here. Nevertheless, there are some common elements of experience for most junior business practice lawyers. Attention to the issues outlined here, therefore, may be a worthwhile starting point for the professional development of a junior business practice lawyer.

Client Focus Is Key

In any relationship with a corporation (or partnership, trust, bank, limited liability company, or other business entity), understanding what the client wants and needs is critical. The form of deal, the outline of potential terms in a negotiation, the aims of new corporate initiatives—all these and more may be important determinants of the business practice lawyer's advice and assistance.

The client's role in a particular transaction, for example, may greatly affect its interest. The junior business practice lawyer must quickly come to learn the differences, for example, between representing a buyer, a seller, a lender, or a financial advisor in a transaction. The client's role in the deal will largely determine the lawyer's role.

Awareness of the client's interest, however, extends well beyond simply asking clients what they want in a particular transaction. A business practice lawyer must strive for a good understanding of the fundamental aspects of the client's business operations, its business model, and its market segment. The business lawyer must be able to anticipate problems based on the client's unique characteristics and offer solutions that work within the client's unique constraints.

Client focus, moreover, includes good communication. The aim of the business practice lawyer should be to keep the client informed and involved in the transaction process at all times. Unlike litigation, where most activities (depositions, court appearances, etc.) will not be handled by the client directly, in business practice it is entirely possible that the client will want to handle large parts of a transaction on its own. The business practice lawyer must constantly inquire whether a particular issue is one that the outside law firm or the client should handle. Fumbling over responsibility for loose ends in a transaction is thus avoided.

The lawyer negotiator must also constantly check with the client to ensure that any problems raised are quickly and effectively resolved. The aim of the business practice lawyer is to develop a reputation as an issue spotter and fixer rather than as a deal killer. Checking in and confirming deal points with a client, moreover, avoids the risk of finger-pointing after a deal closes.

Forms Matter

Each transaction generally has a standard set of documents associated with it that the junior business practice lawyer will be expected to understand and be able to manipulate. These documents typically correspond to the stages of a deal. In a business sale transaction, for example, there may be an initial confidentiality agreement (permitting exchange of information), followed by due diligence request lists and perhaps a letter of intent. Ultimately, there will be a definitive purchase agreement with a variety of provisions (representations and warranties, description of consideration and payment terms, conditions to closing, postclosing adjustment and indemnity arrangements, and many others). Nearly all these provisions may be the subject of bargaining and modification. The junior business practice lawyer must learn the purposes of these standard provisions in order to understand the reasons for, and consequences of, any modification in such provisions.

In their first transactions, of course, it is unlikely that junior business practice lawyers will have frontline responsibility for negotiating major agreements. Junior lawyers are, however, expected to be able to draft revisions to agreements (on instruction from senior lawyers) and to participate in the finalization of documents (filling in blanks, proof-reading and checking for consistency, ensuring that a complete set of exhibits is prepared, and the like). The junior lawyer, moreover, is often responsible for many of the administrative documents on a transaction (deal contact lists, transmittal letters, due diligence requests, closing checklists, and many others). The efficient junior business lawyer has a complete set of forms of such basic documents available for use when-ever necessary.

The junior business lawyer, moreover, must learn the process for commenting on another party's documents (and taking comments on one's own documents). The creation of new drafts, "blacklining" changes, and frequent conference calls and meetings to discuss changes—all are second nature for an experienced business practice lawyer. Junior lawyers, even if they do not have a substantial role in negotiations, must observe the process closely and master the method-ology for efficient identification of issues, positing of proposals, nego-tiation and resolution, and drafting to reflect agreed terms.

Junior business lawyers also learn that there may be large parts of a deal that are beyond their ken. Almost every substantial business trans-action, for example, will have significant tax issues that may have a great impact on the value of the transaction to the client. Many other issues may arise (environmental, insurance, regulatory, employment, and ERISA to name just a few). The problem of arcane deal issues is often particularly acute with cross-border transactions (where legal customs and regulatory regimens may vary greatly from one's native experience). Business lawyers quickly come to learn to spot such unique deal issues in discussions with clients, in due diligence, and in negoti-ations with other parties. When such issues arise, the instinct of the business lawyer must be to avoid playing amateur expert. Often, the most efficient way to deal with an arcane issue is to involve a real expert or local counsel in the deal. At very least, intensive legal research and fact gathering may be required to ensure a complete understanding of the issue and an accurate, adequate solution.

Organization Means Success

The successful junior business practice lawyer generally learns to be superorganized. Awareness of the stages of a transaction and understanding the basic forms may matter little if the business lawyer cannot process a transaction efficiently. The challenges, moreover, may be great. In addition to the on-the-job learning required, junior business lawyers often become involved in deals late in the process and must play catch-up to learn the status of the deal, the client's interests, the problems that have arisen, and the remaining course that is anticipated. Indeed, junior business lawyers may be added to deal teams at the last minute precisely because there is a time crunch to complete the transaction.

In that environment of seeming chaos, uncertainty, and pressure, a junior business lawyer who is not well organized stands a good chance of messing up in some regard. Demands from senior lawyers and clients may come at odd times, often with a "do it yesterday" immediacy. Being organized means being able to follow up effectively on responses to requests that are more long term. Effective junior business lawyers thus are forever making "to do" lists and checking them against their progress. Effective junior business lawyers, moreover, keep their project and form files well organized against the very real possibility that a deal may stop and start again without notice, or an unrelated deal may suddenly call for a form or bit of research developed on a prior deal. With such organization, the experience and increasing judgment that come with passing years may be amplified with effective tools garnered through practice.

The junior lawyer, moreover, may often be tasked with responsibility for cleanup on a deal. Assembling documents into a deal "bible," for example, is often the junior lawyer's job. In addition, the junior lawyer may be required to run down postclosing details and documentation as senior lawyers move on to new deals. Completing these kinds of pesky picayune projects with persistence and attention to detail is part of the junior business practice lawyer's rite of passage into the profession.

WHAT LAW SCHOOL DIDN'T TEACH YOU ABOUT LITIGATION

Law school seems to be all about litigation. You take classes in evidence and civil procedure. Your principal source of information on the law is the casebook, which contains excerpts from judicial opinions in litigated matters. Most often, you write at least one moot court brief, and you get to argue a moot appeal.

Does that make you a litigator? Not exactly. What you must learn in the first few years of litigation practice certainly equals (and probably exceeds) whatever you may have learned in law school. Most of that learning, moreover, is the behind-the-scenes kinds of practical understanding of the litigation process that really cannot be taught well in law school. This section attempts to summarize some of the basic lessons likely to be learned in the first few years of practice as a litigator, and suggests that junior litigators should seek out experience and advice from senior litigators in these and other practical areas of litigation.

The Calendar Rules

Virtually everything in litigation comes with a date or deadline attached. Pleadings must be answered by specific dates; discovery responses are due by specific dates; court conferences and hearings have specific dates. The list goes on and on.

And, in the rare instance where there is no deadline or specific date for an event, your adversary may invent one. Your adversary chooses a proposed date for your client's deposition; your adversary demands that you respond to a settlement offer by a specific date; your adversary requests a "meet and confer" conference on some dispute by a specific date, or he or she will take the matter to court. Again, the list is endless.

Litigators spend much of their time figuring out what dates should be attached to specific events. They consult rules (such as the Federal Rules of Civil Procedure, the Local Rules of the District Court, and the individual rules of the specific judge). They also spend significant time negotiating with adversaries to set, and modify, deadlines. Often, the first contact with an adversary in litigation is to request an extension of time (time to respond to the complaint or time for the initial conference with the court, for example).

For the junior litigator, the habit of thinking about schedules and deadlines must become engrained as early as possible. Often, it falls to the junior litigator to keep track of schedules and deadlines (arranging the deposition schedules of witnesses, for example, or making sure that pleadings or motion papers are served and filed on time).

The junior litigator who assumes that someone else is keeping track of schedules is making a mistake. At a minimum, a junior litigator should be certain of what the dates are for every significant event in a litigation. If there are parts of the litigation schedule that are not within a junior litigator's ken (the schedule for planned settlement discussions, for example), it is generally a good idea to confirm with senior litigators some basic outline of how such schedules might affect the litigation (as in, "If the case does not settle by October 1, then we will have to proceed with aggressive discovery in November and December").

The junior litigator who competently performs the timekeeper role will add real value to most litigation teams. Attention to schedules is

one of the many details that are important in litigation, and for which
senior lawyers will generally be grateful.

Documents Matter

In fiction, most court cases are won or lost on the testimony of
witnesses. The surprise witness, the witness who breaks down on
cross-examination, the witness whose heart-melting testimony sways a
jury—this is the stuff of legal drama in fiction.

In reality, most litigation (especially larger, more complex litigation)
focuses, for a large part of the process, on documents. At trial, of course,
the credibility of witnesses may be critical. But documents often establish the basic facts of a case, because witness memories are deficient. In
addition, the terms of operative documents (contracts and the like) generally determine the major legal issues in the case, even though witness
testimony may amplify or even contradict such documents. Finally,
documents generally matter a great deal because they are hard artifacts
of history. What was written in a letter ten years ago will never change.
What a witness recalls (and how a witness describes) a conversation ten
years ago may vary greatly, as time and circumstances change.

Because documents matter so much, junior litigators must learn how
to handle documents effectively. Mastering the process of producing
documents to an adversary in response to a discovery request is one
critical skill. The process includes learning to communicate with a client
about discovery requests, developing an organized system for gathering documents from a client, and becoming familiar with the conventions (such as Bates-stamping, privilege indices, and confidentiality
stipulations) that are the norms of document production.

Most critically, junior litigators must familiarize themselves with the
rules of attorney-client privilege and work product protection. A significant element of most major document productions is review of documents for privilege and other confidentiality concerns. Junior litigators
are generally expected to at least spot potentially problematic documents (even if they cannot resolve all issues without senior guidance).
Learning to make such privilege calls and learning to ask the right
questions (which of the names on the documents are names of attorneys, when did preparation for the litigation begin, what subjects are
relevant and irrelevant to the litigation) are of critical importance.

In the other direction, junior litigators must learn to piece through
records (from the client, from the adversary, and from third parties) to
learn what happened relevant to the dispute, and to develop the client's
best arguments for the litigation. Junior litigators must also learn to
follow up on leads for additional information. More than simply dupli-
cating prior document requests in other litigation, this follow-up pro-

cess requires attention to detail, noting references to documents in materials already produced and in the testimony of witnesses at depositions. Identifying holes in the pattern of information necessary to establish a client's case and strategizing with senior litigators on how to gather such additional information (from the client, adversary, or third parties) again are essential skills.

Litigators Negotiate Everything

By the time you complete law school, you should be aware that many (if not most) civil litigation matters eventually settle. Despite that fact, many law students take no negotiation courses in law school and may have little practical experience with negotiation.

Effective litigation demands good negotiation skills. But such skills are not simply required for overall resolution of a case. Virtually everything in litigation can be (and often is) negotiated: extensions of time, restrictions on discovery, confidentiality agreements, stipulations of facts, and trial procedures (to name just a few). Junior litigators may be involved in such negotiations at a very early stage.

A junior litigator must be aware that anything he or she says to an adversary (certainly in writing, but also in person or on the telephone) may be construed as a representation of fact or a binding offer to proceed in a particular fashion in the litigation. That fact should make it second nature for a junior litigator to make sure that he or she has authority before speaking on behalf of a client or senior litigator. Where the junior litigator is unsure of authority, moreover, any statements and offers should be expressly couched as tentative, subject to confirmation, or not made at all. The verbal habit, in such situations, is generally to state (in substance): "I hear what you are saying and I will take that back (to the client or senior litigator) for consideration." That verbal habit, of course, must be combined with a habit of promptly confirming (with client or senior litigator) any tentative proposals you may receive from an adversary.

Confirmation of arrangements, moreover, extends to creation of a written record of agreements. The practice of exchanging confirming letters and drafting stipulations and court orders on consent of the parties is an important element of the learning of junior litigators. The process of negotiating and documenting agreements on parts of a litigation, moreover, is part of the preparation for involvement in overall settlement of litigation.

Know Your Audience

In law school, arguments are abstract things, with little connection to actual consequences. Learning to think like a lawyer means developing the ability to think of all sides of an issue. Law school generally does not require that a student pick a side of an argument or focus on persuading a particular audience on a particular point.

Litigators must learn to do precisely that. Starting from the first days of practice, the question of what are the good arguments to be made in support of a client's position in a particular case takes central focus. Potential arguments, even some quite novel, may be vetted in the course of representation, but always with the ultimate goal of determining what is likely to be effective.

Junior litigators soon learn, moreover, that an argument that may be effective with one audience may fail with another. Litigators quickly become aware, for example, of the fact that some clients may love particular arguments, even though there is no way to prove the client's point and no likelihood that a judge or jury would accept the point.

So, too, it is part of the increasing awareness of junior litigators to learn that judges, juries, and (almost always) adversaries may disagree with your best-reasoned arguments. Indeed, junior litigators come to learn that a large part of the value that litigators offer to their clients is the ability to discern which arguments are most likely to be effective in particular situations and to make rough calculations of the likelihood of success with particular arguments. In that vein, the choice not to make certain arguments may be as calculated as the decision to advance particular claims and arguments.

Ultimately, argument selection, order, and phrasing turns on knowing the audience to which arguments are addressed. Junior litigators become accustomed to researching the background of the judges and adversaries with whom they interact. They also learn to tap into any informal networks (colleagues at the firm, co-counsel and local counsel, former classmates, etc.) for information on judges and adversaries. Eventually, when a junior litigator becomes involved in his or her first jury trial, moreover, an acute focus on the characteristics of potential jurors (and the jury panel ultimately chosen) will be developed. Eventually, a junior litigator will find that a great deal of his or her time is spent thinking about, and reacting to, the characteristics of the intended audience (and the likely response of the audience to particular arguments).

There Are Vendors for Everything

Large parts of the litigation process involve tasks that lawyers cannot perform, that they do not do well, or that they prefer not to do. Litigators cannot serve as testifying experts in their own cases (much as they may think that they know everything there is to know on a particular subject). Nor are they particularly adept (in most cases) at handling computer databases and electronic records. And when it comes to organizing and copying paper records, most lawyers would prefer that someone else do the work. In these, and many other instances, litigators can and will engage outside vendors of services to support them.

Junior lawyers must learn to deal with such vendors. The most basic lessons have to do with ensuring that vendor expenses are not incurred without client approval. The learning must quickly progress to the point of giving specific, clear directions to vendors to ensure that the work they do is not wasted or duplicative of work done at the firm or by the client. Ultimately, moreover, the learning extends to the recognition that the ability to assemble a team of players in response to a litigation problem includes the ability to recruit and use outside vendors effectively. Clients largely expect their litigation counsel to handle most of the details in engaging and working with service vendors (although they often wish to know the potential costs associated with vendor services). Establishment of a network of reputable, reliable vendors thus becomes a very useful skill for litigators.

Learning Never Stops

For most litigators, the professional experience is comprised of a series of cases and disputes, each of which may offer the litigator the opportunity to learn some of the basic lessons outlined here, as well as to develop and refine many of the other skills involved in litigation (conducting discovery, drafting pleadings and motions, oral argument, trial work, and more). That learning occurs against a backdrop of exposure to a variety of problems, often in several different businesses and areas of law. Thus, for litigators, learning never stops. Junior litigators must recognize that an attitude of humility ("I don't know much about this problem, but I am willing to learn") will serve a litigator well both in the early stages and throughout a professional career.

5

Ethics and Professional Responsibility

OVERVIEW

Lawyers just starting in the profession rarely think that charges of ethical violations will ever be applied to them. For many junior lawyers, the view is simply "I am on the lowest rung of the ladder, how much trouble could I get in?" Statistics from some jurisdictions, however, suggest that as many as 25 percent of disciplinary committee referrals apply to lawyers with fewer than 10 years of practice experience.

Other junior lawyers simply assume that their law firms have structures (to check conflicts, to maintain separate client accounts, etc.) that will suffice to handle all ethical problems. Yet, any such structures are only as effective as the attorneys working in the firm make them. Further, even if an ethical violation could, or even should, have been identified and resolved by firm supervisors, the disquiet and career blemishes that a junior lawyer may suffer from an ethical lapse are not much reduced.

This section offers some practical suggestions to help ensure that ethical problems do not overwhelm you in the early years of your practice. These guidelines do not focus on the details of ethical rules (which vary from jurisdiction to jurisdiction) and are not based on particularized hypotheticals (the stuff of many ethics opinions and law review articles). Instead, these are general suggestions of ways to avoid getting yourself into trouble and, when trouble appears, for getting yourself out of trouble as quickly and painlessly as possible.

Approach This Subject with Humility

There is a form of self-deception, based in part on hubris and in part on laziness, that takes as a given that "I would never do anything unethical." That "case closed, I don't have to think about this issue" attitude is a ticket to ruin. The subject of legal ethics can be very difficult, with issues and rules that may be much more complex and murky than you think. There are often conflicting authorities on these issues and genuine differences of opinion on what is and what is not ethical. Moreover, there are often powerful incentives (adversaries seeking to gain advantage, disgruntled clients with an axe to grind) for others to raise ethical issues against you, even when you have proceeded in a good faith effort to behave within the confines of the ethical rules.

You are not necessarily well-prepared to address these difficult issues. It is an open secret that professional responsibility is one of the least well-attended classes in law school (often a pass/fail course), and the abbreviated preparation by most junior lawyers for the Multistate Professional Responsibility Examination is generally just enough to pass the test. Further, virtually all ethical rules are tempered to some degree by what is considered normal and reasonable. Both such standards are, by definition, difficult for a new lawyer to know and apply.

Seek advice and consultation early whenever a potential ethical problem arises, rather than try to invent a novel solution to the problem or (worse yet) let the problem drift without any solution until it becomes too big to be solved effectively. In most larger law firms, there is a professional responsibility or loss prevention partner (or committee) who is specifically charged with the duty to address potential ethical problems. Seek the appropriate people out, if need be. Many smaller problems, however, can be effectively understood and addressed by any senior lawyer with sufficient experience. For solo practitioners, consultation with other colleagues may serve the same function. Many bar associations, moreover, offer ethics-related materials on their Internet sites (including solutions to common problems) and may even provide hot-line consultations on ethics issues. At the very least, keep a handy copy of the ethics code that applies in your jurisdiction.

Get Your Own House in Order

A person's life (family, health, finances, work) cannot bear stress in too many areas at once. If you are having a serious personal problem (an elderly parent, a spouse who has lost a job, a child who is ill, and any of dozens of other circumstances that can prevent you from fulfilling your professional responsibilities), deal with that problem before it spills over into your work. You may simply not have time to work on everything that you could handle under normal circumstances. At very least, your attention may be distracted and your judgment impaired. Too often the crisis at home and at work can spiral into other problems (drug and alcohol abuse, depression), which can even further prevent you from functioning effectively. Read a few disciplinary committee opinions. You will often see a pattern that starts with a personal problem and leads eventually to serious ethical violations.

If you are in trouble, ask for help. If you need to take time off or share some work or get some professional counseling, do it. The myth of the lawyer as Superman or Wonder Woman is just that. Part of professional responsibility involves knowing and dealing with your limits. Senior lawyers and clients will generally respect you for dealing forthrightly with such problems. Conversely, if you insist on working at 110 percent when your real capacity is 50 percent, they will rarely be forgiving of lapses that could have been avoided if only you had sought help.

Your Reputation Is Worth More Than Anything

Exercising professional responsibility does not simply mean avoiding inquiry from the disciplinary committee. That should be the least of your goals. The real goal is to uphold the highest standards of the profession in every aspect of your career. Judge yourself as others will judge you—not whether you are generally ethical, but whether each one of your daily activities (any letter to an adversary, any phone call with a client, any representation to a court) meets the standards for ethical conduct.

Building a reputation for ethical conduct starts the moment you enter into professional activity. Even as a summer associate or law clerk, senior lawyers will begin to make judgments about you. Are you trustworthy? When you say that you will get a project done on time, can a senior lawyer rely on you? Are you responsible? When a mistake occurs, will you candidly admit the problem and get it fixed, or will you try to push the responsibility on to someone else? Are you diligent? Do you cut corners and turn in minimally sufficient work on projects you do not particularly enjoy, or do you make sure that all your work, even what may seem like drudgery, is first rate?

Your reputation for ethical conduct will also quickly extend to clients. Any client who observes you engaging in unethical conduct with others (fudging a response to an adversary, advancing an argument you know is unsound) may soon begin to wonder, "If my lawyer is willing to act unethically toward others, how can I be sure I will not be treated the same way?" Indeed, in many instances, clients may come to you specifically for ethical advice. You are a law adviser on many other substantive areas (what does the tax code require; what does a contract provision mean; what are the regulatory issues involved in a deal). The same is true for ethics. Your clients (especially junior level businesspeople or assistant general counsel) will often depend on you to tell them definitively "No, we cannot do that; it is unethical."

Client Confidences Are Key

The very essence of what a client expects from a lawyer is confidential legal advice. Client confidences belong to the client, not to the lawyer. Your first order of business should always be to maintain such confidences, unless otherwise instructed by the client.

The temptations are many. You will be asked by family and friends to talk about your work, and you will be tempted to swell with pride and tell the details of the great work you are doing. Even in the first months of practice, moreover, you may be bombarded with inquiries from recruiters, who seem to want to get to know you. These days, moreover, there are ample outlets (e-mail groups, Internet professional bulletin boards) for complaints and comments about law firm life. You are not precluded from saying anything about your work in these situations, but you are precluded from revealing client confidences. Be careful. The mere fact that you have revealed a client confidence with no intention of gaining any personal benefit will not suffice to repair the breach.

Any misuse of client confidences for personal gain will probably get you in even more trouble. Two words—insider trading—should remind you that trading in securities based on information received in your professional capacity is strictly forbidden.

You May Not Be Authorized to Practice Law

Until you have passed the bar and been admitted, you are not authorized to practice law. Individual jurisdictions may have varying rules on what constitutes the practice of law, but in general you should take all reasonable steps to ensure that no one (not clients, not adversaries, and certainly not judges) mistakenly assumes that you are a lawyer. Frequently, for example, recent law school graduates sign all correspondence with a notation of "admission to practice pending" or "admitted to practice" in a particular jurisdiction only.

Consult with a senior lawyer for directions on this issue. Indeed, it is generally a good idea to consult with a senior lawyer before sending any correspondence outside the firm. Especially during the early years of practice, a quick check with a senior lawyer can help avoid simple errors (misspelled client names, improper format) and may even reveal larger problems (developments in the matter that are unknown to you because of your position). At very least, such check-ins can be learning opportunities, with the senior lawyer giving you pointers on form and substance; such check-ins also help to demonstrate that you are diligently keeping the supervising lawyer informed of your activities.

Be Clear When You Have a Client

Shortly after you enter the practice of law (and perhaps even earlier, while you are in law school), you will begin to receive inquiries from family, friends, and acquaintances, asking you for a little advice or assistance with a legal problem. In many instances, this little bit of advice quickly blossoms into a larger request. Your ear is bent with the details of the person's problem. You may even be asked to take some official action ("Would you mind writing a letter to my landlord?" "Could you call the IRS for me?" "Could you talk to my employer?").

In effect, you are being asked to provide free legal advice and assistance. You may be forming an attorney/client relationship, even though the engagement is unpaid. As a result of the engagement, you may be stuck with the obligation to protect your client's confidences and to avoid conflicts in representation of some adverse client. You may even be stuck with the duty to continue to represent the client, and (worst case) you may be stuck with a claim of malpractice if something goes wrong.

You are not necessarily prohibited from providing free legal advice and assistance, but you must be clear when you have entered into an attorney/client engagement. Most law firms have definitive policies on what is required for approval of any engagement (client conflict clearance, specification of terms of engagement, etc.). If those policies have not been followed, you are asking for trouble. Until you have confirmed that the engagement is proper (by checking the appropriate firm policies and by consulting with a responsible senior lawyer), you should be as clear as possible with the prospective client that you are not undertaking a representation, that you are not accepting confidential information in connection with such representation, and that you cannot commit to provide legal service until the engagement has been approved.

Avoid Charges of Incompetence

No lawyer should purport to have expertise in every area of the law. There will be temptation, especially in a small or solo law firm, to take any work so long as the client can pay the bill. Despite cinematic portrayals of lawyers with no experience who miraculously find a way to win their first case (often a murder case or something similarly dramatic), the reality is that legal expertise generally comes from experience. If you do not have sufficient experience and expertise in a given area, you must refer the matter to an attorney with the requisite ability, or at least make arrangements to associate with such an attorney for purposes of the representation.

You must also be candid with your client about your lack of experience. Do not provide off-the-cuff advice on an issue about which you are uncertain. Tell your client directly, "I am not an expert in this area" or "I would need to do more research to give you a definitive answer." In a larger law firm, especially, seek out the advice of real experts in any area that is unknown to you, and offer to have the real experts advise the client about matters within their ken.

Be careful, also, about taking on a matter where it may be difficult to provide your client effective representation, given the fees at stake. Pro bono clients, in particular, are clients just like any other. If you cannot afford to provide full, effective service on a pro bono matter, you should not take it. Further, you should not quote a reduced fee or budget cap for some legal work where the restrictions will make it practically impossible to do the necessary work.

Consult Frequently with Your Client

If there is one thing that clients hate, it is lawyers who refuse to return their calls and who are not heard from for months on end. This is not just a matter of client relations. Clients expect, and have a right, to be informed of developments in their matters. Clients who are kept in the dark are much more likely to claim (when matters take a poor turn) that their lawyers have acted improperly.

Make it a habit to provide your client with courtesy copies of all relevant correspondence involved in a matter (to you and from you). Some clients may want you to restrict the paper flow, but let the client tell you that; do not simply assume that your client will not be interested in anything other than major developments as you subjectively define them.

Remember, moreover, that you are (at most) merely an agent of your client. You can and should make recommendations; you can lay out the options for your client, but you cannot substitute your judgment for your client's own decisions. In that regard, be especially wary of making representations to an adversary about what your client may do unless you are sure of your client's wishes and you are sure that your client has given you authority to make such representations. There is a clear difference between making a tentative agreement (subject to your client's approval) and stating (in sum or substance) that you are sure that your client will agree to what is being proposed.

Contribute to the Improvement of the Profession

There are many in the law who claim that the profession has changed for the worse. Many see the drive to make the law more like a business than a profession as inevitably leading to a decline in ethical values. Yet, there are hopeful signs everywhere. The profession has replaced some of the worst vestiges of bygone days (overt racial and sexual discrimination) with a developing attitude of inclusion and success based on merit that perhaps could not have been dreamt a century ago. Some of the worst forms of incivility ("Rambo" litigation tactics, for example) have been widely condemned and addressed in new codes of professional conduct. There are many serious efforts underway to provide services to traditionally underserved populations.

These developments, and others like them, deserve your support. Improvements in the reputation of the legal profession are ultimately to the benefit of all in the profession. Start by modeling good behavior of your own. Go farther, however, by contributing (within your law firm, on bar committees, by teaching, through financial contributions, etc.) to improvements in the profession as a whole. Today's junior lawyers will lead the profession tomorrow. Do your part to keep the profession on course.

COURTESY

To be a great lawyer and also a nice person—is that an impossible goal? Public surveys and many popular jokes suggest that the two results are incompatible. Even if many lawyers are by nature unpleasant, should junior lawyers model themselves on the attack dogs of the profession? There are many good reasons for junior lawyers to develop and maintain habits of courtesy and respect as they are learning the more technical elements of their craft.

Make no mistake: Tough times may call for tough action. The lawyer who is generally calm and congenial may, in some circumstances, be required to kick it up a notch, in negotiation or argument. The ability to be assertive, when assertiveness is required, should not be discounted. But if a lawyer starts with a baseline of equanimity, the occasions when emphasis or outrage are expressed may have even more effect than the constant state of aggression (even hysteria) expressed by some lawyers.

In the give-and-take of a lawyer's world, moreover, a background of trust and good faith may be essential. Some suggest that only transactional lawyers need to foster a cooperative spirit to get a deal done. But even in litigation there are many occasions where horse-trading and accommodation are required. You want the deposition of my principal witness; I want your documents. You need to postpone a filing due to the press of other work; I know that I cannot try the case on specific dates because of family commitments. Deals must be struck, or the parties will waste time and money on motions and court conferences.

Indeed, unbending inability to compromise may stand a lawyer in terrible stead with adversaries and judges. To report to a client that no deal was struck, even if covered with a bravado "take no prisoners" attitude, may be worse then reporting that a deal was struck on terms that are less favorable than the client had expected. Worse, in the litigation arena, an obdurate manner may lead to much worse results before a court than might have been achieved through compromise. Indeed, the lawyer who consistently maintains extreme positions may cause a judge to question the legitimacy of every position, even if some are well-taken.

Even though some clients may openly state their desire for a "killer" lawyer to represent them, that attitude may fade when the lawyer's hyperaggressive style precludes completion of a deal or settlement of a lawsuit. Indeed, it must occur to many clients, eventually, that a lawyer who uses unrestrained tactics in dealing with adversaries may use the same tactics in dealing with clients. That very thought may cross a client's mind as he or she reads a billing statement listing countless hours spent on filing near-frivolous motions or fighting over every last jot and comma in a deal document.

Within a law office environment, moreover, development of a reputation as a jerk may be deadly. Senior lawyers avoid juniors who are distinctly unpleasant, no matter how brilliant or dedicated. Even if they do work with them, the peppery associate may get none of the war stories, gossip, and advice that can come from a friendly affiliation with a senior lawyer. Senior lawyers do not generally like to mentor junior lawyers who are jerks.

In the junior ranks, braggadocio may also have an extremely adverse effect. Law firms operate on teamwork. The over-the-top junior lawyer may find it very difficult to get advice from compatriot juniors, much less find another junior to cover an assignment when the inevitable time crunches arise. Law office staff (secretaries, paralegals, photocopiers, etc.) may also be much less than enthusiastic, and may even subtly sabotage projects, for junior lawyers who have reputations as screamers, or worse.

Ultimately, moreover, there is the personal side of a life in the law. What does it profit you if a brilliant career is littered with the remains of a lifetime of bitter, unpleasant encounters? Worse yet, it is difficult to adopt one persona at work and another in family and social relations. The lawyer who sets as his or her goal to become the toughest on the block may be in for a lifetime of wrecked relationships and loneliness.

Here's to the nice lawyer—one whose professional goal is not to annihilate all adversaries and competition but to provide good quality services and reasonable solutions to client problems, and who (in the process) enriches his or her family and community. Nice lawyers can (and should) finish first.

PROMOTING DIVERSITY

Diversity serves the legal profession well. The business community, as with the population in general, is increasingly diverse. So should the legal profession be. Indeed, if anything, the profession should be a model for employers in other arenas. If the legal profession is to be involved in enforcing antidiscrimination laws, it should also itself be able to observe such laws and demonstrate the benefits of employing a diverse workforce.

Such aspirational goals for the profession must be implemented by lawyers involved in the management of law firms. In a real sense, however, development of a diverse workplace requires the dedication of each individual lawyer in the profession to the vital task of promoting diversity and ridding the profession of the vestiges of discrimination and prejudice. This section suggests some of the steps that every lawyer can take in this regard.

Take Advantage of Existing Resources

Although the profession is far from perfect, the resources dedicated to the promotion of diversity are substantial. Take advantage of these resources to educate yourself and to make it possible for you to respond effectively to the many challenges that may arise in this area.

Start with your own law firm. Many firms have some basic training in employment issues (how to combat harassment in the workplace; how to respond to employee grievances; these and many other topics may be covered). Take the basic training, but seek out more of what the firm may offer. Is there a diversity committee? Is diversity one of the issues addressed by the recruiting committee? Who are the individuals responsible for responding to complaints of harassment or other employee grievances? Once you discover these resources, spend time learning what structures and programs already exist in this area within the firm. To the extent that you can, moreover, offer your own suggestions (and your time) to help improve the firm's response to issues of diversity.

Seek out resources beyond the firm. Most bar associations have committees involved in diversity issues. Many law schools sponsor programs to help educate the profession in this area. Many other social and political organizations are involved in education and advocacy. Take advantage of such resources to learn more on the subject but also to make connections with people who are focused on improving the profession's performance in this area. Often, their experiences and insights may be as valuable as the awareness training that may be provided by law firms and other organizations.

Set a Personal Example

In an era of political correctness, it is tempting to proclaim, "I would never discriminate" or "I am not prejudiced," but mere mouthing of platitudes is not enough. What is required is that we all show real dedication to this issue. There should, for example, be zero tolerance for racist, sexist, or other offensive jokes and similar behavior in the workplace. Avoid such behavior in your own practice, and do not encourage or even tolerate it in others. As part of educating yourself about diversity issues, learn to identify comments and behaviors that may be offensive to others. When you observe any such behaviors in your colleagues or subordinates, gently (but firmly) remind them of how the behaviors may be offensive. Of course, there will be circumstances where camaraderie and good cheer seem to sanction banter, but even there offense can occur. Practice a policy of "When in doubt, don't."

When a colleague or subordinate complains of offensive or intolerant behavior, moreover, take the matter seriously. Be a good listener in encouraging the person to explain what has happened rather than dismiss what may on the surface sometimes seem to be a trivial or transient incident. Encourage the person to seek advice and assistance from the managers at the firm responsible for human resources, diversity, and discrimination issues.

Consider what other steps you can take to foster diversity and tolerance at the firm. Examine your own practices in recruiting, in mentoring, and in staffing the matters for which you have responsibility. There is a natural tendency to prefer to work with people who are most like yourself. Counter that tendency with the recognition of the enriching value to be gained from working with and learning about a person whose culture may be different from your own. Do not assume that it is someone else's job to embrace and integrate people who may be different in some way from the mainstream of the firm's working population.

Speak Up

Law firms can be intimidating places, and there is a temptation to believe that you have to go along to get along. But silent suffering will not bring change (at your firm or within the profession as a whole). If you are the victim of harassment, discrimination, or any similarly unfair employment action, raise the issue with the appropriate authorities at the firm. In most instances, you should find them willing to listen and eager to ensure that such actions do not recur. If you do not encounter an appropriate response from one of them, try another.

If you discover aspects of firm practice that are not necessarily discriminatory but that are less than effective in promoting diversity, speak up about those as well. Although there should not be a presumption that the only people who care about diversity issues are lawyers who may come from different backgrounds than the mainstream of a law firm, it is true that such lawyers will often have unique insights and suggestions about diversity-promoting practices. Be prepared to share such insights, if you have them.

The old adage "If you are not part of the solution, you may be part of the problem" applies to this problem as much as it does to any other. It is not appropriate simply to grumble about how poorly the firm treats its lawyers. If you have specific suggestions, make them. If you are not sure who should get the suggestions, find out. If there appears to be difficulty finding someone to implement the suggestions, offer to help out.

RESPONDING TO "RAMBO" TACTICS

The problem of "Rambo" tactics can be frustrating at any stage in a legal career. For the junior lawyer especially, confrontation with an adversary who engages in abusive, profane, condescending, dishonest, obstreperous, or perhaps even unlawful conduct can be particularly challenging. A junior lawyer may not have enough experience to be certain of what is normal, and what is required or permitted under applicable rules. A junior lawyer may also not have complete knowledge of the facts of the case (perhaps because the supervising lawyer has assigned only a slice of the matter to the junior lawyer). In either event, the junior lawyer may not feel confident that his or her position is well grounded and certainly may not feel confident enough of that position to call a more senior lawyer on some shoddy tactic. The temptation, all too often, is to suffer in silence rather than to risk a confrontation.

The problem is further complicated by the junior lawyer's status. A junior lawyer may not have enough client contact to be sure whether the client will want to spend time and money sending letters, making motions, or taking other steps to discipline unruly adversaries. The junior lawyer may also be uncertain as to how a judge will react to claims of unfair or abusive behavior. The junior lawyer may even fear that complaints about an adversary could backfire and cause a client, a court, or a supervising lawyer to view the complaining junior lawyer as a whiner.

For some junior lawyers, this maddening scenario, where an unscrupulous adversary runs roughshod, with the junior lawyer feeling powerless to respond, can be enough to make the first few years of practice distinctly unpleasant. Is there any good solution to the problem? To some extent, the solution is time. Eventually, with experience, even the most junior lawyers will begin to recognize that just because a more senior lawyer engages in a practice, the practice is not necessarily right, or fair, or tolerable. In addition, however, here are a few suggestions to help organize a junior lawyer's response to "Rambo" tactics.

- Pay attention to your own reactions to the behavior of other lawyers. When you begin to have an emotional reaction (like rage or frustration) in response to an adversary's conduct, the little voice inside you is telling you that something is not right. Focus on what the other lawyer is doing that strikes you as unfair and that makes you want to fight back. If you ignore your own reactions, you are headed for trouble. The feeling will likely get stronger with time rather than go away. Moreover, the abusive lawyer who gets away with an initial ethical breach will be tempted to do it again, and again. Eventually, when you explode, it may be out of proportion to the specific item of conduct, simply because you have tolerated abuse for too long.
- Report unprofessional behavior to senior lawyers on your team or in your office as soon as possible after such behavior occurs. You will likely gain confidence from the reactions of a senior lawyer, confirming that the conduct you find unfair truly is inappropriate, and you may receive helpful suggestions on how to deal with the conduct. You will also avoid the fear, later in the case, that if you bring some peccadillo to a senior lawyer's attention, you risk the senior lawyer either dismissing the particular problem as trivial or (on learning of a pattern of problems) saying, "Why didn't you tell me about all this before?" Ultimately, because dealing with unprofessional conduct is part of the overall strategy in a case, senior lawyers should be kept in the loop because they need to be able to advise the client on the current status, and next steps, in the litigation.
- Try to stay calm, even in response to outrageous conduct. If you are in the heat of battle (in a deposition, for example), you may want to take a break before continuing. If you are drafting a letter or motion related to the conduct, take some time to cool off before

you send it, or file it. Your reaction to bad behavior should be clear, focused, and professional. In the aftermath of a confrontation, you will want to make sure that you can hold your head high and say, "I treated my adversary with courtesy and respect. His/her improper conduct is entirely his/her fault."

- Feed back to your adversary in precise, measured terms exactly what it is that you consider to be unprofessional behavior. In a deposition, for example, it may be necessary to state, "Sir, you are shouting at my witness. I want you to stop immediately, or we will suspend the deposition and seek assistance from the court." Similarly, in a telephone conversation, it may be necessary to tell an adversary that cursing and threatening is unprofessional. If the behavior continues, the telephone call may have to be terminated.
- Make a record of improper behavior as soon as it occurs. Such a record (a statement in the transcript of a deposition, a letter confirming the substance of a telephone call, etc.) may help greatly in any application to a court. Such a record may also help to deter unprofessional behavior. Videotaping depositions can be an especially effective method of deterring abusive or unfair conduct that would not be captured on a "cold" transcript. In some egregious cases, with adversaries who engage in persistent misrepresentation or abuse, it may be desirable to cut off all communication other than in written form. Even the threat to do so may be incentive to the unprofessional attorney to shape up.
- Become familiar with the terms of relevant disciplinary rules and standards of procedure, such as Fed. R. Civ. P. 11 (sanctions for frivolous or harassing pleadings and motions); Fed. R. Civ. P. 37 (sanctions for discovery abuses); 28 U.S.C. § 1927 (sanctions for unreasonable multiplication of proceedings); and local and state court rules. Citation of such provisions in communications with adversaries can help show that you are well versed in applicable rules and that you are serious about your lack of tolerance for improper behavior.
- Take advantage of your junior status where possible. The innocent question may be, "Gee, Mr./Ms. Smith, I didn't know the rules permitted that action. Can you tell me where you get authority to do that?"
- If possible, take advantage of your junior status with the court as well. Where the facts are clearly stated, few judges will fail to understand that some senior lawyers may try to bully a lawyer who is new to the profession. Getting a judge on your side as a counterweight to such bullying may be a tremendous advantage, not just on the particular disciplinary point but in the litigation as a whole.

- Be absolutely intolerant of comments that have racist or sexist overtones. These kinds of comments are generally easy to identify. Courts and disciplinary committees have quite appropriately taken lawyers to task for any such comments, regardless of the supposed excuse.
- Model good professional behavior of your own. Keep your promises. Do not engage in cheap shots. Be prepared to stake your professional reputation on your every action, every day. Act like a professional, and you can reasonably expect to be treated like a professional.

Despite watching years of television and film portrayals of lawyers who indulge in ethical lapses of every stripe, many junior lawyers are quite shocked the first time such tactics are turned in their direction. Sadly, it is almost inevitable that such behavior will be encountered sooner or later. The junior lawyer must be prepared to confront the "Rambo" lawyer calmly but firmly. Formulation of a plan aimed at preventing such behavior from recurring, once it first arises, is half the battle.

6

Time Management

AVOIDING STRESS AND BURNOUT

Articles on lawyer burnout and stress often recite the characteristics of a lawyer in trouble: lack of interest in work, isolation from friends, irritability, persistent exhaustion, irresponsibility, anger, cynicism, and negativity (to name just a few). Commonly cited culprits in creating these conditions are crushing billable hours and increasing demands from clients. Such articles often suggest that lawyers facing stress and burnout cut back on work and consider major lifestyle changes. Often, the articles include success stories about lawyers who work part-time or who have moved to far-off small towns where clients are somehow friendlier and the work somehow more fun.

For many lawyers, such fantasy solutions ("quit working so hard" or "quit your job and go work somewhere more fun") are so unrealistic that lawyers ignore the problem altogether. Indeed, many lawyers pride themselves on how stressed and miserable they are. Say the word "workaholic" and their heads swell. Say the words "drunk," "addict," "mentally ill," "divorced," or "quit the profession," and they think of some "other" losers who were not tough enough to take it. In short, because the problem seems to have no practical solution or because they simply are not aware of (or do not want to think about) the problem, for many lawyers the question of how to avoid burnout, stress, and all the other symptoms that may come with them is never addressed.

Worse yet, for many lawyers, once the effects of stress and burnout become obvious, to themselves and their colleagues, their ability to rectify the imbalances in their lives may be too limited to permit recovery without a radical break from work or some other intrusive intervention. Withdrawn, irritable, and afraid, attorneys suffering from stress and burnout may turn to drugs or alcohol to ease their pain, or they may simply give up on the responsibilities of their profession. Indeed, many lawyer assistance programs work on the assumption that lawyers who take advantage of such programs will do so because they are too impaired to work professionally and may be jeopardizing the affairs of their clients and their law firms.

Are those the only choices available for dealing with stress and burn-out: either ignoring the problem or waiting until the horses have left to close the barn door? What if the problem were put in more practical, immediate terms? Ask yourself: If you had an argument in court tomor-row morning, or an important client meeting, would you try to get a good night's sleep? If you had some document review or due diligence for a few days in Anaheim, would you try to have a night free to visit Disneyland? If you just had a major fight with your spouse over the tele-phone, would you wait a while before making a call to a client?

Obvious as they may seem, these are precisely the kinds of questions that busy lawyers may forget to ask themselves. Occasional failure to pursue such commonsense means to avoid stress, boredom, and ex-haustion on any given day probably will not hurt you. Persistent inattention to the problem, however, can have devastating conse-quences.

Stress and burnout avoidance requires regular, if not daily, attention. Just as a diet and exercise program can help you lose weight, establish-ment of a plan for stress and burnout avoidance can help get you to incorporate behavior changes that can be comfortably incorporated into even a very busy attorney's daily routine.

A few basic principles deserve mention.

- Nobody else but you can, or will, take responsibility for this problem. Your coworkers and friends will not make you diet, exercise, or go to the doctor, and they will not make you do this either. *You* must have the will and the desire to affect your own behavior in healthy ways.
- Relief from stress and burnout will not come tomorrow unless you do something about them today. Lawyers are great at rationalizing and even better at deferring rewards. Both characteristics can be tickets to gradual but inevitable breakdown.
- Mere quantity of time away from work is not the solution to all stress and burnout problems. Indeed, the idea that time off is somehow a miracle cure may be part of the problem. Stressed-out lawyers who take unsatisfying vacations only to return to work feeling no better than when they left may conclude (wrongly) that there is simply no hope for solving this problem.
- A key element of stress and burnout prevention is some soul-searching, aimed at identifying things that truly make you feel

happy and refreshed. The goal is to see how many of these things you can incorporate into your daily routine and still have a successful career. Some of these things may be very brief (5 minutes of quiet time or meditation each morning, a 20-minute jog three days a week, or reading a few stories to your kids each night before bed). The point is that daily, brief, quality experiences may be as valuable as less frequent vacations.

- Do not knock vacations, however. Not only are they a great way to recharge depleted mental batteries, but thoughts of vacation past, or vacations planned, can be enjoyed as brief respites from a busy day.
- Aside from searching for quality-time experiences, some of the best methods of stress and burnout avoidance involve efficient time management. Many management advisors, for example, suggest doing the hardest task you expect to do at the beginning of your day (when your energy and enthusiasm are likely to be at their highest). Similarly, prioritizing work, keeping a careful calendar, and learning to delegate effectively can all help to avoid the "permanent crisis" condition that some lawyers create.
- The nature of your law practice will rarely change as much as your reaction to the practice. Something drew you to law in the first instance. What was it? Look for those elements of your practice that are most satisfying to you, and spend time thinking about how you can maximize such experiences. If you do not find such satisfying things in your daily life as a lawyer, perhaps you need to restructure some of the work you do, or consider taking on some pro bono, teaching, or other outside occupation to spice up your working life.
- Pay careful attention to your reactions during times of maximum stress. If you are upset, tired, and anxious and feel at your wit's end, take some action, immediately. Get up, take a walk; go to the gym; do some yoga; listen to some soothing music; call your mom. Whatever works for you, have some safety net that you know will always help make you feel better when you are truly down.

There are many popular books and other resources on mental well-being that are well worth reading for ideas on creation of an individual plan to avoid stress and burnout. Many bar and CLE groups conduct seminars on the subject. Most mental health professionals, moreover, are eager to consult both for prevention purposes as well as for treatment of acute problems.

Formulation of a specific plan to avoid stress and burnout will help ensure that vague hopes to take it easy some day do not give way to a working life of boredom, tension, and chronic unhappiness. Mastery of basic stress and burnout prevention techniques may be as important as other essential lawyering skills (research, writing, negotiation, etc.) for long-term success in a legal career.

THE HOME/WORK BALANCE

In a bygone era of traditional family roles and standardized working environments for lawyers, there was perhaps little need to dwell on the question of how to balance the demands of home and work. Work, for most lawyers, came first, and home a clear second. If you did not care to follow that priority scheme, you simply did not enter the field of law.

Today, the law is much more open to lawyers with a variety of concepts of how to balance home and work. This new working environment presents the challenge of how to find a balance that makes most sense to you and that is practical in your circumstances. This section outlines some of the factors to consider in striking your own personal home/work balance.

The Need for Balance

Begin with the recognition that some balance is inherent in the practice of law. Despite increasing flexibility in working arrangements, law remains a challenging, demanding profession. Just as law school can occupy essentially all your waking time if you let it, so too can the practice of law potentially demand as much time as you are willing to give.

Yet, there is clearly some need for balance. If you have no life outside the law, you may endanger your mental, physical, and emotional health. Maintenance of a home life (broadly defined to include maintaining family and personal relationships, and other activities outside of work) is essential. Your successes may be more satisfying and your challenges less difficult to bear if you have time to share them with someone at home. Indeed, for many lawyers, there is little point to a successful career if there is no satisfying nonwork life. Moreover, for many lawyers, the demands of home life (such as caring for an ailing family member) simply cannot be ignored.

At the other extreme, unwillingness to compromise on home priorities may make it impossible to pursue the kind of vibrant, fulfilling practice that you desire. There are some "punch the clock" law jobs available, but they are rarely as desirable as jobs where schedules are less structured (and thus where more time demands are presented).

Establishing Priorities

The sense that many lawyers have is that, because the demands of law are potentially limitless, the challenge in finding a home/work balance is to figure out when to say "No" to work. That method, however, is bound to overestimate the value of work and underestimate the value of home. Far better to take each component as presumptively equal in value and then determine circumstances in which the value of one clearly outweighs the other.

Your top priorities will likely be one-of-a-kind events (for both home and work). Your wedding or the birth of your first child will almost certainly be much more important than any work experience. Your first trial or your first major solo deal by contrast, may be worth many late nights that crowd out regular home events.

Within these extremes, virtually every home or work activity can be placed on a continuum of priorities, and a rough equation between home and work established. Your priorities, of course, are your own. Your priorities may change over time and may vary with circumstances. Yet the key analysis will not. The choice to work is a choice not to spend the same time at home, and vice versa. Getting your priorities straight on this issue does not mean that you will reach any particular result, but that you will remain conscious, at all times, of the fact that you are making choices.

Setting Limits

Once you have thought through your priorities, the next key element in any plan to establish an effective home/work balance requires making sure (on both ends) that you set limits that ensure that your priorities are recognized by those around you (at work and at home). The more that those around you know how you wish to balance your home and work priorities, the easier it will be to achieve your preferred balance.

Start with your secretary. Your secretary should know your priorities, on a general basis, and should, as a result, be in a position to help you implement your plan. Your secretary should, for example, be able to inform your colleagues and supervisors of your whereabouts and schedule at all times and quickly transmit messages to you when you must be away from the office. In the other direction, your secretary may be able to help you organize your work in such a way as to ensure that all your working time is efficiently spent, thus increasing the time you can spend at home.

The same goes for announcing your priorities to others with whom you work. The more they know about your schedule, in a general sense, and even on a day-to-day basis, the better off you will be. If, for example, you know about a significant home event in advance, you should take steps to announce your expected absence from the office (and, if appropriate, make arrangements to have a colleague cover your desk during your absence). If there is a regular element of your home schedule that will keep you away from work, you should let your colleagues and supervisors know about that constraint. In the other direction, if there is a routine element of work (a regularly-scheduled Monday morning meeting, for example) you should let those at home know that you must conform your home schedule to that requirement.

Be as specific as possible, in both directions. The vague request of your employer that you want to cut back on hours for some period, for example, will be much less effective than the request that you be able to leave the office each day at 5:00 P.M., or that you can only work four days per week. It may be that you need to negotiate specific arrangements with your firm, but your mutual understanding of the arrangement will be far clearer, and your ability to stick with your imposed limits far easier, than if the discussion about arrangements is not specific.

The discussion at home should also be specific. Vague promises that you will try to spend more time at home cannot be effectively implemented. Be realistic about your needs, and clear about your plan. Avoid the frustration that can come from the sense (express or implicit) that the demands of those at home are somehow interfering with your career. If you are clear about what your home priorities are and you take steps to ensure that those priorities are honored, your home discussions will center on how best to balance home and work under the circumstances, and not whether your home life holds any priority for you.

Having It All

There are no magic choices. Every decision involves some trade-off between home and work priorities. If you set as your goal the impossible standard of having it all, you may be setting yourself up to fail.

Fortunately, in our modern work environment, it is much more possible to conceive of compromises and life plans that permit more balance than could ever be achieved in the bygone era. Today, for example, most law firms have some form of part-time work program (and even, in many firms, programs to achieve partnership and perform as a partner on a part-time basis). Most firms, moreover, are increasingly embracing second-career and older lawyers, making it possible in many instances to attend to home life for a period and then return to full-time work when appropriate. The concept of having it all thus now extends to an entire career. Thus, the notion of a home/work balance is not confied to any particular point along the path of a career. The result is greater flexibility and greater opportunity to formulate a plan that is right for you.

PLANNING THE USE OF YOUR TIME

Life is what happens in the spaces of time while you are waiting for something important to happen. Or so it may seem in a law firm. Even for busy junior associates, the truly big events in a working day may be relatively few. There are the occasional meetings with senior lawyers, phone calls or meetings with clients, and events outside the office (such as court conferences or negotiation sessions). Much of the rest of the time, however, appears to be free, at least in the sense that you do not absolutely have to do any particular thing at any particular moment.

Indeed, at most law firms, there is really no requirement to punch a clock or account for your every activity throughout the day. So long as you get your work done (and bill sufficient hours) you appear to be free to work as you please.

But are you truly free? With even a little experience at a law firm, it becomes apparent that you cannot conduct your activities in a truly careless or chaotic manner. Your efficiency and your well-being may be jeopardized if you do not place some structure on the use of your time. This section aims to touch on some of the methods of time structuring that may be effective for you. These general ideas, of course, are just that, and they may require modification to suit your particular situation.

Time Priorities

On any given day, there are some things that you absolutely must do, some that you would prefer to do (if you have time), and some that it would be nice to do (but that you can, in theory, put off indefinitely). In simple terms, these are high-, medium- and low-priority items.

- High-priority items tend to have immediate, significant effects. Preparing for and attending a client meeting, for example, is likely to be a high-priority item.
- Medium-priority items tend to have significant effects, but their immediacy may be more limited. Organizing documents for a deposition that is to take place in two weeks, for example, is likely to be a medium-priority item.
- Low-priority items have very long-term, more limited effects. Keeping up on reading of journals in your area of interest, for example, may be relatively low priority.

This priority ranking immediately suggests some structure for your use of time. High-priority items may be the only things you work on in a given day. When they are not, at very least you will want to ensure that all high-priority tasks associated with a given day are accomplished. Some time management experts, for example, suggest that you should begin working on your highest-priority task soon after coming to work (if possible), and make sure that any high-priority tasks are completed before you move to anything else.

That form of response to high-priority tasks is not absolutely required. But it is important to have some sense of priorities and some method of keeping tracking of them. Some experts, for example, suggest using some written system to keep track of your priorities. A simple "to do" list may suffice. Listing all the tasks you expect to perform during the day, prioritizing them, and then adding to and subtracting from that list during the course of the day may help you to put your priorities in concrete, recognizable terms. For many people, creation and use of such a system can provide real confidence that it is possible to gain control over what might otherwise be a very hectic, frazzled work experience.

At a minimum, keeping a calendar of upcoming activities will permit you to account for the events that you absolutely must attend, and the tasks that have specific deadlines. The extent of the detail in such a calendar is up to you, but having some regular system of recording your schedule, and sticking with the process of keeping track of major new events and activities and modifications in your schedule, is vital.

Interruptions and Reordering

Maintaining a rough priority scheme for your time, moreover, permits you to deal with interruptions and sudden reordering of priorities. Interruptions may occur in many forms (the surprise telephone call from a client, the sudden call down to a partner's office for an impromptu team meeting, and many others). You should plan for such likely events and learn to deal with the effects they may have on your priority scheme.

So, too, events in a day may overtake your priority scheme, and require reordering of priorities. In a call with a client or in a meeting with a partner, for example, you may be assigned new tasks with relatively high priority.

When interruption and reordering occurs, you should have some system to adjust your time management. Here are a few suggestions for how to respond.

- Collect your thoughts whenever there is a transition in your day (an interruption or reordering event). The temptation may be to plunge immediately back into your work to counteract the feeling that you are behind. But that way constitutes an abandonment of time planning and may lead to mistakes in prioritizing. Spend at least a few minutes reviewing your work priorities before starting back to work.

- Find the rhythm of your personal style of work. Perhaps you work best in the morning. Try to schedule your highest-priority work for that time and avoid interruptions (if possible) during that period. If interruptions arise during that period, moreover, consider whether it is best to go back immediately to your prior activity after you have dealt with the interruption. Conversely, if there are particular times in your day when you know it will be impossible to attend to high-priority work on a concentrated basis, plan your high-priority work for another, more effective time if possible.
- Consider whether some interruptions and rearranged priorities can be avoided through better communication. Keeping in periodic contact with clients and senior lawyers at times that are most conducive to accomplishing your work priorities may avoid interruptions and sudden reordering of priorities at inopportune times.

Daily Rituals

It has been said that the only things that are important in life are the things that are done every day. A professional's day must include certain daily rituals that are important to long-term success. Treating these rituals as low priority can mean that they are rarely done and eventually are ignored altogether. Here are a few common rituals that you may wish to incorporate into your daily routine:

- Handle administrative matters. Do your daily time-sheets. Chat with your secretary for a few minutes to make sure that he/she knows your plans and needs. Spend time cleaning off your desk and in-box. File. These are only a few of the administrative matters that you may wish to make a daily priority.
- Attend to your health. Go to the gym or find some other form of exercise you can do regularly. Eat a healthy lunch. Get up and stretch periodically. Meditate or take a short nap if you need one. Again, this list is hardly exhaustive or necessarily right for you. The point, however, is that you are not an unbreakable machine, and you will function much better if you are physically fit.
- Maintain personal contact. Call your clients and potential clients periodically, of course, but also keep up with friends and colleagues inside and outside the firm. Make dates to see your old classmates. Take time to stop by the offices of lawyers in the firm

when you know, but with whom you do not always work. These
kinds of activities can keep you energized and stimulated, and in
many instances can lead to informal networks that can be very
helpful to your career.

- Plan some fun. Even a few minutes every now and then spent
  planning something fun (an office party or other event, or a personal vacation) can give you a breather from a hectic day.
- Do some good. Putting even a small part of your efforts into
  activities that you view as beneficial to the communities to which
  you belong (at the firm, within the profession, in your neighbor-
  hood, at your religious institution, within your family, or wherever
  else may be important to you) will make you feel good. Such
  efforts, moreover, over time can lead to real improvements in your
  surroundings.
- Fill in the gaps. Think of some of these daily rituals as potential
  gap-fillers. When you are waiting between meetings, conference
  calls, and trips, can you do some of these things? If so, the time will
  not be wasted, and you will be more effective.

These suggestions, of course, are ideals. We all have crazy days where
schedules are destroyed by events and work drags on seemingly forever. Those days should be exceptions, not the rule. Planning your days
should make it possible to do more, and feel more enthusiastic and
fulfilled, than simply reacting to events or living in factory-like drudgery. Your time is largely free for you to shape. Your challenge is to use
that freedom wisely.

7

Office Relations

INTRODUCING YOURSELF TO SENIOR LAWYERS

There is a classic question in philosophy as to whether it is better to be good or to be thought good by others. In the context of a law firm, the practical answer is that both elements are critical. The focus of this section, however, is on the latter point, getting the "face time" with senior lawyers necessary to let them come to know who you are and to appreciate your value. Assuming that you are a competent, committed junior lawyer, how do you make sure that senior lawyers (and ultimately clients) recognize your worth? Conversely stated, how do you make sure that senior lawyers will not ignore you (except when you have messed up or they need something from you)?

Start with the understanding that most senior lawyers are busy people who generally must prioritize their days so that they can do what needs to be done. Indeed, in the high-speed world of many law firms, the drive is often to eliminate as many things as possible from a given day (documents that do not need to be read; phone calls and e-mails that need not be answered, at least not immediately). Add to that the normal family and social obligations of life, and it may come as no surprise that many senior lawyers will, in fact, ignore junior lawyers unless they have a reason not to do so.

Next, recognize that it is often not the length of contacts with a senior lawyer that is important; it is the quality and frequency that will determine the senior lawyer's impression of you. You can spend an entire day with a senior lawyer (at a negotiation or closing, or at a deposition or a trial). If your contact with the senior lawyer is not meaningful, some senior lawyers may not even remember your name after the experience. By contrast, if a senior lawyer sees or hears from you on a regular basis and each time learns something valuable (or at least has a pleasant experience with you), then the senior lawyer will almost inevitably, over time, form a favorable impression of you.

Assuming that these basic principles make sense to you, the practical implementation of the principles should be fairly obvious.

- Pay attention to your general level of interaction with senior lawyers in the firm. Do you spend all or most of your days in your own office? Have you shared a meal with any of the senior lawyers in your group? Do you have some basic understanding (from them) of what kinds of work and what kinds of clients occupy these senior lawyers? Do these senior lawyers have some basic understanding (from you) of your talents and interests? Do you know something about their personal lives (and vice versa)? Obviously, you need not be a social butterfly, but you should adopt a general goal of having at least enough contact with senior lawyers in the firm to avoid feeling isolated and out of step. You can mark your progress toward that goal by answering some of the practical questions just mentioned. Generally, however, the more frequent and positive your interactions with senior lawyers, the better.

- Assign yourself responsibility for providing senior lawyers with whom you directly work periodic updates on what you are doing for them. The function of such updates is generally to make sure that the senior lawyer knows what you are doing so that the senior lawyer can give you directions if necessary. From your perspective, however, such updates can have a number of ancillary benefits. Best case: The senior lawyer recognizes the vital assistance you are providing (and may even tell you so). Intermediate case: The senior lawyer approves what you are doing, perhaps with some additional directions (or more work assignments). Such an encounter is at least an implicit recognition of your value. Worst case: The senior lawyer tells you that you are doing something wrong. Although the encounter may not seem positive, often the senior lawyer will at least give you credit for seeking supervision. At the very least, early exposure of the mistake is far preferable to later (where the senior lawyer discovers your error and calls you on the carpet for it).

- Make sure that the update is meaningful and as brief as the senior lawyer wants it to be. Often a pop-in to the senior lawyer's office will suffice ("I'm almost finished drafting the XYZ Complaint"; "Jones called—I'll call him back today"). If a face-to-face report is not possible, the same message by telephone or e-mail may be adequate. Such a message could be coupled with the offer to provide more information if the senior lawyer wants it and at the senior lawyer's convenience. Avoid long monologues in the senior lawyer's office. If the senior lawyer only has time for a five-second update, give that and get out. Let the senior lawyer invite you to stay to give more detail (and be prepared to give that).

- If the senior lawyer does invite you to stay or if you find yourself in a circumstance where a senior lawyer must spend time with you (as in waiting for a flight at an airport), be prepared to make that encounter comfortable and positive. Focus on the reality that most people (and certainly most lawyers) are somewhat egotistical. They love to talk about themselves. Use the opportunity for personal contact with the senior lawyer to express an interest in what the senior lawyer does. If the time is limited, ask about the background of the project: What else is going on that might relate to the specific work that you are doing? If you have more time, ask more generally about the client or the kind of project in which you are both engaged. If you have relatively unlimited time, perhaps you will get into the senior lawyer's background: How did he/she decide to become a lawyer? What is the most interesting work he/she has done as a lawyer? How does he/she balance life as a lawyer with family and social obligations? The list of questions is endless. The answers to these kinds of questions, moreover, may spark further discussions the next time you have an encounter with the senior lawyer. Eventually, moreover, after sharing some of this kind of discussion, most senior lawyers will also express an interest in you (your background, your goals, etc.).

- Once you have made real contact with a senior lawyer, assess whether it is something positive that you want to pursue. There may be some people that you do not want to spend a lot of time pursuing (because they are not much involved in any of the work you do or want to do; or because there simply is no good chemistry between you). If the contact is something you want to pursue, make sure not to fall off the map after your first encounter. Even if the specific project ends, assign yourself the responsibility for periodically checking in with the senior lawyer ("Is there anything else I can do on this matter?" "Is there anything else I can do for you generally?"). You may also take note of developments (cases, legal articles, etc.) that could be of interest to the senior lawyer. Dropping off such materials could be the occasion for developing work on the next assignment. At very least, senior lawyers will get the basic message that you are interested in what they do and that you want to work with them again. At very least, every time you see the senior lawyer again (walking by in the halls, at a cocktail reception, etc.) take the time to stop and reconnect ("Whatever happened to that project?" "How are things with [X] client?" "What have you been working on recently?" "How is your family?").

- Do not say no to any reasonable request from your preferred senior lawyer contacts, at least at the outset of your relationship. One of the most positive attributes that senior lawyers ascribe to the junior lawyers with whom they prefer to work is availability. If a senior lawyer gets the impression that you will always make the time to help out on one of his or her projects, the senior lawyer will almost inevitably consider you to be one of the first people to call whenever there are new work assignments. This impression should not be conveyed without some limits, of course. If you truly are too busy to handle a new matter for a preferred senior lawyer, then you should say so candidly. Even in that situation, however, you may be of value. You could suggest another junior lawyer who could help out, or you could offer to do only part of the work or to join in the work at a later point when your schedule lightens. In any event, the message is the same: You are here to help the senior lawyer in any way possible under the circumstances.

There is no magic bullet in developing good relations with senior lawyers. No single encounter will make or break a relationship. Paying attention to the development and cultivation of such relationships will, however, over time make the difference between a world where work is imposed on you by unknown and uncaring senior lawyers and a world where you participate actively in the affairs of the law firm, your group, and the senior lawyers with whom you work. Ultimately, development of solid relationships with senior lawyers will also improve your ability to be selective about the kind of work you do and may improve your chances for advancement to partnership.

DELEGATING WORK

From the moment you enter a law firm, you are a manager. At first, you may do no more than manage support staff (your secretary, word processors, the copying department, and others). You manage by delegating parts of your work to them. Your effectiveness and efficiency depends, in large part, on how well you delegate.

As you gain seniority and experience, the ability to delegate effectively becomes ever more important. You begin to handle several projects at once; the projects become more complicated; and the circle of persons to whom you delegate work becomes ever wider.

Most lawyers, however, never receive any formal training in management. Law schools do not generally teach the subject, and most law firms expect on-the-job experience to suffice. As a result, among the most universal complaints in law firms are those related to delegation.

Senior lawyers often complain that "you just can't get good help any more." Junior lawyer complaints are more like "I hate working for [Joe or Jane partner]. He/she is always in my face or I can't find him/her for days at a time."

A Delegation Self-Test

Ultimately, in a law firm, the only person you can really manage is yourself. You need to think about how you deal with work that is delegated to you and how you delegate work to others. The first step is to become aware of some of your own behavior that may be impeding effective delegation.

Ask whether any of the following statements is true for you:

1. You often complain about the work habits of your subordinates, but they never seem to improve.
2. You have piles of paper on your desk, consisting of work you plan to get around to, but never seem to do.
3. You are certain that no one can do your work as well as you can; if you were not around, mistakes would be made or critical steps would be left undone.
4. You often find yourself getting work from senior lawyers at the last minute, with unreasonable deadlines.
5. You get assignments from others that you do not understand or that seem nonsensical to you.
6. You feel like you are not learning anything new and are doing the same kinds of work over and over.

If any of these statements rings true with you, you may have a delegation problem. The question is not whether you work with jerks and incompetents or whether you might fit in better at some other law firm. The question is whether there is anything you can change about the ways you get and give work that may make you more efficient, effective, and satisfied.

The Concept of Delegation

What is delegation? Most fundamentally, delegation involves sharing work. A decision is made that some parts of a project will be performed by one person, and other parts performed by someone else. For legal projects, there can often be multiple delegations, with several people working on various aspects of a project.

Effective delegation requires a good understanding of the project. At least one person needs to understand the object of the project and its component parts. There must also be an understanding of the capabilities and availability of the other person(s) to whom work will be delegated.

Productive delegation also requires good communication. The person delegating work must describe the background of the project adequately and give instructions that are understandable. The person taking on the work must clearly feed back an understanding of the background and instructions and identify any constraints (lack of training, time, or other resources) that may impede completion of the assigned task. The parties involved must teach each other about their needs and negotiate the terms under which the work will be performed.

What Work Should Be Delegated

Effective delegation starts with the question "Why am I doing this work?" On reflection, you may discover that some work need not be done at all. Someone else may already be doing the work. The need for the work may have been superseded by events. In some instances, the work may simply be a matter of habit or custom that serves no real purpose.

It is also important to remember that delegation does not always go down to subordinates. In many instances, a senior lawyer or even a colleague at your level has more training or experience in a particular area than you do. Often, the efficient way to get particular work done is to delegate up (or sideways) by picking the brain of another person with knowledge or by handing off the work wholesale.

In addition, there are several key characteristics of work that may be effectively delegated. Look for assignments that

1. involve repetitive, routine work in areas where your repetition of the work will not improve your skill or understanding.
2. have a low risk of errors or can be easily fixed if an error occurs.
3. require only a working, not perfect, knowledge of the overall project, such that the time required to explain the background of the project will not overwhelm the efficiency of the delegation.
4. will permit a subordinate to learn an essential skill or to become more acquainted with the work you do, such that the assignment can become an opportunity to teach the subordinate how to assist you on other projects.

These are not the sole hallmarks of delegable work, of course, but a thorough application of even these most basic criteria will very likely yield a substantial list of candidates for delegation of work.

Tips for the Assigning Lawyer

The ideal delegation of work involves giving a person just enough information and authority to make sure that they can effectively complete the assigned task and learn from the experience. Lack of information and authority is bound to lead to bad results. If you do not tell a person enough about the project and your requirements, you can expect either indecision (and repeated, annoying demands for more instructions) or wasted effort and mistakes. Similarly, if you do not give a person enough discretion and authority to complete the task with some independence, you will produce inefficiency and frustration.

With these general guidelines in mind, consider the following suggestions for improving the effectiveness of delegation:

1. Make sure that the lawyer to whom the work is delegated is right for the job. If the lawyer has few of the required skills and experience for the work, success may be impossible. On the other hand, it may be possible to match the lawyer's skills to some subpart of the work, permitting a more limited, but successful, delegation.
2. Make sure that the delegation dialogue is two-way. Try to ask as many questions of the persons to whom you assign the work as they ask of you. Do they understand the assignment? Do they have any experience related to the assignment? Do they foresee any problems in taking on and completing the assignment? What steps do they plan to follow in carrying out the assignment? What do they plan to do first?
3. Make sure that you have agreed on the most fundamental terms of the delegation, such as: When is the work due? Do you want to see the work in draft or only the finished product? Do you want progress reports? Are there any areas related to the work that you do not want touched? Does anyone else need to be consulted in connection with the work?
4. Offer any resources that you know are readily available to help complete the assignment: Is there any precedent form or relevant prior research? Has anyone else in the firm ever done this kind of project? Is there a major treatise or standard reference that can help? Are there any firm policies that might affect the project?
5. Make sure that any time constraints imposed are reasonable and real.
6. Do not pull the plug as soon as something goes wrong. With most assignments, some mistakes will inevitably be made. Patient effort to understand the problem and to help the other lawyer solve it is an essential part of the learning experience that comes from delegation.

7. Build in some system for feedback on the project: Set a specific time, if possible, to discuss the work, any additional assignments that might grow out of the work, and any suggestions for improvements (in both directions) in the future. For larger projects, with several attorneys working on various tasks, it is common to have a regular team meeting or conference call to discuss the progress of the work. Even for smaller projects, scheduling a specific time to discuss what has gone right and wrong with the work may help to ensure that the work gets done on time and that learning opportunities from the assignment have been exploited.

Tips for the Receiving Lawyer

Delegation does not come easily for a lot of lawyers. Moreover, in the rush of busy working days, taking the time to delegate effectively may not seem attractive to some. As a result, the lawyer receiving an assignment in many instances must do double duty: performing the actual work and also performing the work involved in making sure that the delegation goes smoothly. It is tempting, in the receiving role, to throw up one's hands in frustration when the senior lawyer does not delegate well. Yet, there is often little satisfaction (and even less after-the-fact recognition) in knowing that work was flubbed because the assigning lawyer did not pay attention to his/her role in the delegation.

Consider the following suggestions for improving the way in which you receive delegated work from other lawyers:

1. Always give the delegating lawyer some kind of summary of what you understand of the matter, the overall project, and your specific assignment, no matter whether the delegating lawyer asks for it. If it is not possible to give that summary at the point of the initial delegation, make a point of looping back (an office drop-in, a telephone call, an e-mail) to give that summary.
2. Look for ways to break the assignment down into smaller parts in order to report your progress as you go. Periodic reports on completion of the smaller parts of the assignment will reassure the delegating lawyer that you are paying attention to the assignment and will allow correction by the delegating lawyer if any part of the assignment has been misunderstood. If possible, make those reports face-to-face or at least live on the telephone. Stealth messages left in the middle of the night often produce more confusion and annoyance than they save. Try to give your first progress report as early as possible to maximize the chances of getting additional useful directions early in the course of the project.

3. Be especially careful before taking a major step (one involving significant risk to the client or significant cost or time) that you have not discussed with the delegating lawyer. Try to identify such major steps as early as possible in order to give the supervising attorney ample time to review the steps you plan to take. Avoid the situation where you have to invent consent from the delegating lawyer (as in, "I'm sorry; I thought I told you I was going to send that material out if I did not hear from you by Friday.").

4. Report delays and other problems as soon as they arise. Belated confession that something has gone wrong risks the delegating lawyer's (often extreme) irritation. A prompt acknowledgment of the problem, together with presentation of a suggested solution, shows courage and concern.

5. Do not subdelegate significant parts of your assigned work without telling the assigning lawyer. The assigning lawyer picked you for the job and expects you to be responsible for the results. If the assigning lawyer knows and approves of the subdelegation, of course, further sharing of work may be entirely appropriate.

Overcoming Barriers to Delegation

As noted, perhaps the principal problem preventing effective delegation is the lack of training that most law schools and law firms provide in this area. For the busy lawyer who may not have received formal training in this area, a quick review of any of the popular management advice books will probably yield some useful insights. There are also beneficial seminars and on-line courses on the subject.

The central message of many of these courses is that delegation is something to be embraced for its benefits rather than feared for potential loss of control. Junior lawyers who are actively involved in projects, who feel that they are learning and stretching their abilities, are generally more productive and satisfied. Senior lawyers who can let go of less important tasks find that they can focus more on strategy, client contact, and business development, among other more satisfying activities.

The recognition that delegation can be a win/win situation for senior and junior lawyers may not suffice to establish a culture of effective delegation. Among the more basic problems are these:

1. There may be a lack of familiarity with the abilities of lawyers to whom work may be delegated. Senior lawyers need to take affirmative steps to familiarize themselves with the talents and interests of the junior lawyers in their firm. Junior lawyers need to take affirmative steps to advertise those talents and interests to their seniors. There is no magic formula for getting to know each other.

Many firms use regular office cocktail parties and department meetings as well as mentor/mentee programs in an effort to promote social interaction beyond the bounds of the single work assignment.

2. There may be a lack of confidence in the training and experience of the lawyers to whom work may be delegated. Senior lawyers need to make sure that the training and work experiences offered to junior lawyers are appropriate to the needs of the firm. Often, the best way for senior lawyers to do that is to offer to teach in-house seminars on their own areas of practice. Junior lawyers need to take responsibility for ensuring that they are getting the training they need to succeed. That means taking advantage of in-house training when it is available, but also paying attention to potential learning resources outside the firm.

3. There may be a perceived lack of encouragement to have junior lawyers take on ever-increasing levels of responsibility. Senior lawyers need to set goals for the experiences that junior lawyers should have as they progress through their careers. Periodic counseling sessions with junior lawyers can help to ensure that their career progress is on track. Junior lawyers need to mark their own progress, and to speak up when they see potential opportunities for work that could significantly expand their experience base. Junior lawyers also need to recognize that the career experience of a lawyer is cumulative and progressive. A junior lawyer does not suddenly come to know everything about a chosen field upon making partner. Steady effort to acquire skills and experience is what leads to success before partnership and beyond.

Find Your Own Style

Delegation is an art, not a science. Each practitioner has a particular style, and no single style works for everyone. Yet, effective techniques for delegation can be studied. In the modern law firm, with compartmentalized structures and functions, the ability to delegate well is essential. Indeed, client demands for efficient lower-cost legal work essentially correlate to a very real need to delegate work effectively. A focus on development of the art of delegation is well worth an attorney's time, no matter the attorney's age or status.

ACCEPTING RESPONSIBILITY

Perhaps some of the most amusing segments of sports blooper programs are those depicting two baseball players chasing a fly ball, where the players collide, or miss the ball, as an apparent result of miscommunication. To avoid this kind of on-field fiasco, coaches at every level of the game (from peewees to the pros) tell their players that they must signal which of the players will pursue the ball. Shouts of "I've got it!" are commonly heard on the baseball field.

In the multitask world of sophisticated legal service, the same problem can arise. When two lawyers each assume that the other is performing a task, the task may never be done, or it may have to be performed out of sequence under time pressure. When two lawyers each assume that he or she is responsible for the same task, duplication and inefficiency can result. In either event, effective completion of the project may be impaired, relations among the lawyers may suffer, and, in some instances, serious professional embarrassment (at the very least) may occur.

The obvious solution to those kinds of coordination problems is good communication among the lawyers on a practice team. The problem, from a junior lawyer's perspective, is that quite often senior lawyers may hand out what appears to be a fairly specific assignment only to chastise the junior lawyer later for doing too little or too much on the assignment. Following are a few guidelines (from the junior lawyer's perspective) that may help to avoid this problem.

Begin with the initial assignment process. Recognize that most senior lawyers, concerned for efficiency and strapped for time, will tell you just enough about a project to permit you to perform the assignment. They may not tell you what work has already gone into the project, who else is working on the project, what the others are doing, or what other steps are contemplated. You must investigate these questions, either by asking the assigning lawyer in the first meeting or in subsequent communications with the assigning lawyer and others on the project team.

You must also be completely candid about your skills and experience and any time constraints that may affect your ability to complete the assignment in a timely and effective manner. If you have never drafted a document of the kind involved in the project, say so (and ask for help finding an appropriate precedent—recognizing that any precedent may need to be adapted to the specific circumstance). If you are not familiar with the law in a specific area, say so (and ask for advice on the law or direction to an appropriate text so that you may become more familiar with the area). If you have other work that may affect your ability to complete the assignment, say so (and be prepared to either lose the assignment or to share it with another lawyer). If these kinds of problems appear after you embark on an assignment, moreover, you must report the problem to an assigning lawyer well before the problem begins to impair your performance.

Recognize also that many senior lawyers will assume, once you have undertaken an assignment, that you are working on it and that you will complete it on time and in good form without further direction unless needed. If you do not receive reminder calls or memoranda from assigning lawyers, do not assume that they no longer care about the assignment. As with clients who repose trust in their lawyers to take responsibility for a project and handle it, you should take full responsibility for any assignment you get from a senior lawyer without the senior lawyer having to remind you of that responsibility.

Taking responsibility also means putting full effort into every assignment. Unless you know of specific constraints on the work (and you should ask about these), you should not assume that a first draft, preliminary research, or a work-in-progress analysis will suffice. Nor should you assume that a senior lawyer will catch any mistakes that appear in your work product. If the work is incomplete, if you have made assumptions about the facts, or if you are unsure whether your analysis is correct, tell the senior lawyer that you have taken your best shot at the problem, but that you have some reservations (and clearly indicate what those reservations are).

In the opposite direction, if you see a problem in the work product or analysis of another lawyer on your team, do not remain silent on the assumption that they must know what they are doing or that they will fix the problem later. There are few things more frustrating to senior lawyers than to be told late in the project that some obvious error occurred, but no one fixed it because everyone assumed that someone else was responsible (this is perhaps the classic equivalent of the dropped fly ball). In particular, if you discover in the course of an assignment that the directions you got for the assignment no longer make sense, you must tell the assigning lawyer about the problem. Wasted, counterproductive work may be worse than no work at all.

The general rule in case of any question about an assignment must be that more communication is better than less. Thus, periodic updates to supervising lawyers about what assignments are on your plate, your progress on the work, any problems encountered, and any scheduling issues should be the norm. Whether these updates take the form of team meetings or conference calls organized by the supervising lawyer or reports you devise on your own (regular drop-in visits to the senior lawyer's office, telephone calls, e-mails, memoranda or updated "to do" lists), the point is that you should make sure that supervising lawyers are aware of what you are doing (and not doing) for them.

There is, of course, the danger that too-frequent messages and questions about your work may be perceived as annoying or a sign of lack of independent ability and initiative. There are some essential rules that may avoid that result. The bigger and more irrevocable the problem, the more critical it is to get direction. If you are sending a document outside the firm (to a court, an adversary, or a client), for example, it should generally be in the best possible form (accurate, complete, proofread). Most often, you should make sure that it is reviewed by a more senior lawyer. Further, the less certain you are about the facts, the law, and the purpose and implications of your work, the more you should seek confirmation that you are proceeding correctly.

If possible, try to time and phrase your messages so that they will have maximum value and minimum annoyance. A message left on a supervising lawyer's voice-mail at midnight on a Friday vaguely referring to a problem that you need to discuss before a client meeting on Monday morning is virtually guaranteed to bring forth a negative response. Be specific about your work and any problems. Outline your proposed solution and any alternatives that may exist. Let the supervising lawyer know how and when you can be reached. Most important, speak up as soon as you know that you need direction rather than wait for events to demonstrate that you have a disaster on your hands.

Finally, recognize that many senior lawyers, once they have you working on one assignment for their project team, may assume that you are on the team for all purposes. That may mean, at a minimum, that you should expect to receive additional assignments beyond the scope of the original assignment related to the project. Such continuing work may be a very good thing, as you get to see a project from start to finish and expand your competence by taking on new responsibilities.

You should also be aware, however, that some senior lawyers may assume that you are fully versed in the role of the junior lawyer and that you will handle all the details of the role essentially without any direction. These situations are true traps for the unwary. Some senior lawyers will grade you as inferior (in their own minds and perhaps even in a formal review) merely because you did not understand that they expected you to do more than respond to a specific assignment.

Again, the solution is forthright communication. If you tell a senior lawyer that you have never worked on a particular type of project before, that you know nothing about the law in the area, or that you have other assignments that will limit your ability to handle the project, your chances of being unfairly labeled incompetent or inattentive may be dramatically decreased. Similarly, if you see that some important task on a project is not being performed, inquire of the senior lawyers to determine whether they are assuming that you will manage the task.

Finally, a word of caution for the future. These "Who's got it?" problems do not disappear after the first years in a law firm. If anything, they multiply. The higher you move in the pecking order of the firm, the more difficult it may be to say who should be doing what on a project. The good organization and communication skills you develop as a junior lawyer will become even more critical as your career advances. Mastery of such skills at an early stage may be one strong indicator of likely future success.

KEEPING IN TOUCH

Imagine your secretary answering your telephone as follows: "Oh, hello Ms. Jones. No, Mr. Smith isn't in the office yet. He didn't tell me when he'll be in this morning. No, I'm not sure whether he's working on your document. Would you like to leave a message?" Can you guess what kind of impression Ms. Jones is likely to form from this kind of exchange?

The solution to this problem (and many others like it), to avoid the very likely negative impression that could result, is to keep in touch— with your secretary, with your colleagues, and with your clients. This chapter focuses on a few practical tips for developing and maintaining a system to keep those with whom you have professional contact aware of your schedule and availability.

Start with your secretary. He or she can be a critical ally in this process. Your secretary should know where you are and how to reach you at all times, and should know what to do in handling inquiries in your absence.

This does not mean that your secretary should be calling you constantly when you are away from your office. Your secretary should know enough of your schedule and your priorities to determine which inquiries require an immediate response and which can be held for a spare moment (and when those spare moments are likely to occur). Your secretary should also know your habits in retrieving messages. Perhaps you prefer that your secretary collect messages and read them to you over the telephone when you call in. Perhaps you prefer to have all the messages left on your voice mail. Perhaps you routinely pick up remote e-mail (by handheld device for example). The point is that your secretary should know which method you prefer and should use that method exclusively so that you do not need to check each potential source each time you are away from your office.

Consider also your colleagues, including those both senior and junior to you. One key aspect concerns any document that you may receive that should be shared with the rest of your practice team. In most instances (unless the documents are extremely bulky or you have been told not to circulate certain categories of documents), you should consider it part of your responsibility to ensure that soon after you receive an important document, other members of the team have the same information.

Fortunately, technology and a little organization can make this task relatively simple. You should be able to provide your secretary with lists of the members of your practice teams and provide your secretary with either standing instructions, or a note on each document, authorizing circulation of the document to your team. Faxes can be easily forwarded for this purpose. For larger documents (and document collections), you may want to inform the team (by e-mail or otherwise) that the documents are available for copying if members of the team want them. Some firms, moreover, make use of scanning devices, at least for certain types of documents.

Another key aspect concerns your schedule, especially at critical times (such as vacations, due dates for major documents, or important meeting dates). Your team needs to know in advance when you will not be available and (if possible) what plans you have made to cover your other work when you are not available. It will often be possible for another member of the team to handle your duties in your absence. It may also be possible for you to plan to check in regularly to handle your duties from outside the office, or to give occasional attention to other tasks, even as you are focused on a major project. Your team members need to know, however, what method you are using to cover your assignments and whether there are some tasks that they will need to address on their own without waiting for your input or approval.

The notice of your absence should be adequate for your colleagues to understand the circumstances and any need for action on their part. Avoid last-minute notice and vague references to "call my secretary if you have any problems." The longer the expected absence, the longer the notice period should be. Provide several reminder notices for any particularly extended absence, which will almost certainly produce some disruption to the work of your practice teams. Some firms, moreover, have systems to list personal calendars in a space available to all lawyers. Consider using such systems as an additional source of notice.

Finally, consider your clients. One critical aspect concerns responding to client inquiries. You should make it a habit to answer every client telephone call no later than by the end of the day that it is received (and much sooner in the case of urgent calls). When you are absent from your office, your system for retrieving messages must be functioning effectively at all times. Your secretary must have some method to make it easy for any client to leave a message and to receive your response. The more your secretary knows of your schedule and when you are likely to return the call, the easier it may be to get a quick response to your client and to senior members of your practice teams. If your secretary knows who is handling a matter in your absence, moreover, the client may be able to get an immediate response from another lawyer in the office. When other arrangements cannot be made, you may also have your secretary encourage the client to leave a detailed message, which you may answer as soon as you become available.

Keeping in touch with your clients, however, is not merely a matter of responding to questions. Clients are entitled to periodic updates on the progress of your work and any significant developments in their matters. Depending on the nature of the assignment and instructions from the client, you may need to provide your client copies of all documents pertinent to the matter. At a minimum, you must inquire as to what documents (or types of documents) your client may wish to review. As with internal circulating lists, your secretary should have complete address, telephone, fax, and e-mail details for purposes of circulating information to your clients and should be careful as to when and how to send materials related to an individual project. Changes in the circulating list and special instructions regarding circulation of certain information should be carefully discussed with your secretary to avoid embarrassing mistakes and omissions.

Despite your best efforts to keep in touch inside and outside your office, there will be circumstances when your system fails. In some instances, the fault may not be your own (clients and senior lawyers, for example, may fail to take notice of your vacation plans despite repeated announcements). In other instances, your own failures may be the cause of the breakdown (such as when your secretary does not know your daily schedule or does not get updates to your client contact lists). In each instance, the frustration that may arise should provide you with motivation to improve your contact system and to maintain it more regularly. Your efforts, moreover, will often be rewarded with the appreciation of clients and senior lawyers who will come to expect that they can rely on you to be in touch at all times. That expectation is both the benefit and the burden of mastering this essential professional skill.

WORKING FOR A JUNIOR BOSS

For many new associates, the experience of beginning practice in a law firm is filled with anticipation. At last, the academic world can be left behind for the real world of the full-time practice of law. For many, part of the anticipation is the hope to connect with experienced senior lawyers, who can serve as mentors and teachers, guiding the new associate toward mastery of the profession.

The pleasant anticipation, however, may soon give way to a stark reality: Many senior lawyers delegate much of the responsibility for supervising the most junior lawyers on their teams to midlevel associates. The most junior lawyers may feel cut off from the mentoring and teaching they had expected. Worse yet, new lawyers may chafe under the directions of the junior bosses for whom they largely come to work.

This section aims to describe some basic strategies for working with, and for, the junior boss. Naturally, individual circumstances in individual law firms may vary. These strategies are, therefore, only suggestions to be adapted, or rejected, as need and conditions dictate.

Clearly Define Your Goals

In many instances, the first reaction to the imposition of a junior boss is the desire to escape the situation. The sense that "I didn't sign up for this arrangement" often takes hold. Yet, it is almost never possible to escape entirely from being subject to junior bosses. The junior boss system is part of the culture of most large law firms (and even many medium- and small-size firms). In many instances, it is a highly efficient way to staff projects.

If it is not possible to escape the junior boss system, then what should be the new associate's goal? The original goals (mentoring, teaching, and recognition) should remain firmly in sight. Instead of attempting to escape the junior boss, however, the new associate must think of ways to attain those goals through, and with the assistance of, the junior boss.

Give the Junior Boss Some Respect

The junior boss almost certainly will not be an ally if your essential attitude is one of disrespect. In many subtle (and sometimes quite direct) ways, many new associates essentially tell their junior bosses, "You don't know anything" or "The partner is my real boss, not you." These spoken and unspoken messages are a grave challenge to most junior bosses, who may be quite anxious about their own abilities and status. Such challenges are often met with great annoyance (if not hostility) and can seriously impede the communication process.

An attitude of basic respect ("I acknowledge that even though you are only a year or so ahead of me, you know more about this project than I do, and you are responsible for supervising me") is best. That basic respect is not an invitation to abuse; it is an invitation to proceed as two junior professionals to make the most of your relationship.

Communicate Your Wishes

For many junior bosses, the experience of supervising a new associate may be one of their first real experiences as a manager in the law firm system. In many instances, the main focus of the junior boss is to accomplish the tasks at hand. Although junior bosses may desire more intangible goals for themselves (status and recognition in the law firm, for example), they may not think of themselves as having some responsibility to help you attain such intangible goals for yourself.

To enlist the aid of a junior boss, you will need to communicate as clearly as possible your goals for your working relationship. Such a conversation (more likely a series of conversations over the course of one or more projects) usually begins with a simple request for information. "Can you tell me more about the background of this project?" "Are there some basic documents I can read to gain more understanding of the client and this problem?" "Is there any good basic text that describes the law in this area?" These kinds of questions are nonthreatening and generally indicate that you are interested and enthusiastic about the project. The response from the junior boss, as a result, is likely to be positive.

The more in-depth conversations that follow may take you down many paths. The junior boss may know a great deal more than you know about the area of law, the specific type of project, the client, and the senior lawyers involved in the project. Asking questions in any of these areas, all against the basic background of respect for the junior boss and an expressed desire to contribute to success on the project, is often the foundation of a mutually beneficial relationship with the junior boss. That relationship will often transcend the individual project as the junior boss begins to think of you as a "go to" person who can be relied upon in many other situations.

Be Independent, within Limits

Although the relationship with a junior boss may be mutually beneficial, it can at times become suffocating. The junior boss who demands all your time may make it difficult for you to establish relationships with other lawyers in the firm and may cut you off from a broader range of experiences and competence. Again, direct and clear communication on the issue may often be best. "I want to work for a variety of people." "I want to see many different styles." "I want to introduce myself to as many lawyers in the firm as possible." Any of these are reasonable, neutral messages, not designed to insult the junior boss but to articulate your needs and desires.

Participate at a Higher Level

Many new lawyers, for all their complaints about junior bosses, find it easy to work with a junior boss because the new lawyer appears to bear less ultimate responsibility when all work is filtered through the junior boss. In essence, the new lawyer who is a pure functionary is less at risk for a mistake in judgment. By remaining in the purely subordinate role, however, the new lawyer decreases the opportunity for exposure to the most senior lawyers on a team and decreases the opportunity to develop skills and experiences beyond the introductory level. The solution, in many instances, is to push information up beyond the level of the junior boss.

Where possible, seek to participate in team meetings and conference calls where all phases of a project are discussed and senior lawyers on the team may be encountered. Your understanding of the project will be deepened, and your ability to advertise your contributions to the project enhanced. When you report in writing on your progress, moreover, try to include more members of the team than just the junior boss. In informal settings in the office (social functions and chance encounters in the halls, for example) do not hesitate to tell senior lawyers something about your work. Keep all lines of communication with senior lawyers open. When asked to take on more responsibility by a senior lawyer, moreover, jump at the chance.

Remember, however, to keep your connections with the junior boss intact. The point is not to leap over the junior boss but to demonstrate that you can participate in the functioning of the team with increasingly less supervision from the junior boss. As a result, the junior boss should be freed for other, high order tasks.

Do Not Forget Your Roots

Progress from new lawyer, just walking in the door of a law firm, to junior boss, beginning to serve as midlevel manager, is often remarkably rapid. In short order, you will confront many of the same challenges that your own junior bosses confront. Keep in mind some of your own frustrations as a new associate in this circumstance. Listen to the new associates who work for you. Reassure them (if you can) that you are willing to help them through the process of beginning a career in a law firm. Take pride in your ability to carry on the tradition of mentoring, even at the most junior levels.

THE AIDE-DE-CAMP ROLE

In military history, the aide-de-camp role is well recognized. During the French and Indian War, George Washington was an aide to British General Edward Braddock. During the American Revolution, a young Alexander Hamilton was one of General Washington's aides. George Patton, before he earned distinction in World War II, was an aide to General John F. "Black Jack" Pershing in his skirmishes with Pancho

Villa. For each, service to a great senior commander was a critical early stage in forging a successful career.

In law, as in the military, there may come opportunities to serve as an aide to a senior lawyer. When it works well, the aide role can be highly beneficial to both the senior and the junior lawyer. When it goes wrong (or goes on too long), however, it can ruin the start of a good career.

More Than a Functionary

An aide does not simply work in the same area as the senior lawyer. Typically, the aide is the "go to" person on most of the senior lawyer's projects. Other lawyers in the firm know it; clients know it; and opposing counsel know it. When the senior lawyer is not available or does not wish to handle the details of some project, they all know that the aide can be relied upon to make decisions and speak for the senior lawyer or at very least to gain the senior lawyer's attention to resolve any issues that require senior judgment.

The senior lawyer thus gains a middle-level manager who can keep the project moving with relatively little direction. The aide also serves as a filter, anticipating and resolving problems where possible and bringing only the most important unresolved matters to the senior lawyer for consideration. Finally, the senior lawyer may use the aide to gain "plausible deniability," trying out views without the senior lawyer's express imprimatur. Such tentative views may be modified or abandoned by the senior lawyer, depending on the response.

More Than a Mentor

For the aide, a senior lawyer is often much more than a mentor. The senior lawyer is a teacher and role model, giving the aide an inside look at effective lawyering techniques and unique opportunities to participate in higher level strategy and project planning.

The senior lawyer's choice of an aide may also have significant indirect benefits in the aide's career. The aide may be introduced to clients and senior lawyers inside and outside the firm under circumstances that would not otherwise be possible. The aide, moreover, may be groomed for future leadership. The senior lawyer often becomes invested in advancing the career of his or her protégé.

Trust and Responsibility

In the medieval military origins of the role, the aide-de-camp was responsible for bringing orders from a commander to his troops. No more vital mission could be entrusted to a young aide.

The hallmarks of an aide, in the law firm setting, are also trust and responsibility. The senior lawyer entrusts the aide with authority. The aide, cognizant of that trust, must take all necessary steps to make sure that the senior lawyer is kept well-informed of important issues (the facts, the arguments, and the stakes) and that any decisions the aide makes on important issues are a substitute for the senior lawyer's judgment, not the aide's own concept of what might seem best.

What Senior Lawyers Want

The ideal aide, as noted, should have a keen sense of responsibility. More than that, an aide should be discreet, capable of handling difficult situations with maturity and tact. An aide must, for example, be able to deflect (with grace and appropriate toughness) any pesky adversary or client who insists on dealing only with the senior lawyer. Similarly, the aide should be especially adept at listening to and asking questions of clients and adversaries so that the senior lawyer need not fill in major information gaps when he/she steps in to direct the project.

An aide should be organized, having all the pertinent facts concerning the project (telephone numbers of clients and adversaries, schedules for proceedings, status of various elements of the project) available whenever the senior lawyer needs them and whenever the senior lawyer has time for a briefing on the project. Successful aides often employ things like "tickler" or checklist systems to keep track of issues and to brief the senior lawyer in the most efficient manner.

An aide must be continuously available, ready to fill in for the senior lawyer with little notice. An aide must be flexible, taking calls and meetings at odd hours and doing extra, "hurry up" work whenever required.

An aide must spend time doing the extra homework on the projects, on the clients, and on the area of practice that can make the aide an especially competent assistant. Service in the aide-de-camp role can offer a unique opportunity to "strut your stuff." If the aide is not a quick study, however, the benefits of that unique opportunity may be lost.

Because the aide spends so much time with the senior lawyer, the aide must be likable, pleasant, and easygoing. A good sense of humor is a plus. A genuine personal interest in the senior lawyer's career is also essential.

When Things Go Wrong

The ideal of the aide-de-camp role is probably rarely achieved in a law firm. Most law firms have too many lawyers and too many different kinds of clients and projects for any single senior lawyer to dominate a single junior lawyer's time completely. Nevertheless, for some junior lawyers, in some firms and some practice groups, for some periods of time, the aide-de-camp role is a real option. A senior lawyer may, for example, appoint an aide for a particular large project or a particular client. That kind of limited appointment of an aide-de-camp happens quite frequently.

Should the junior lawyer take on the aide role? To some degree, the question cannot be answered, because it is impossible to predict whether a relationship will work until the relationship has begun. A junior lawyer may, however, be able to learn (from former aides and other lawyers in the firm) what it might be like to serve in the aide role with a senior lawyer and what former aides report on their experiences with the senior lawyer.

Most fundamentally, if the senior lawyer does not demonstrate a basic level of trust and respect for his/her aides, the relationship should be avoided. The senior lawyer who turns an aide into a servant, assigning menial, uninteresting tasks, is abusing the aide's loyalty. The potential benefits (unique learning and experience, prestige, and confidence building) will also be lost.

Similarly, the senior lawyer who totally dominates the relationship may also be a problem. The aide who becomes known solely as the likable sidekick (à la Gabby Hayes and Roy Rogers) may never grow out of the role. Here, perhaps the best predictor of the potential success of the relationship is the senior lawyer's track record. Have junior lawyers who worked for this lawyer moved on to become full-fledged lawyers in their own right? If not, or if they have all had to leave the firm or practice group in order to do so, then serving in the aide role with this particular senior lawyer may create problems for a junior lawyer.

Finally, there may be some senior lawyers who like to work principally with one aide for reasons that are not work-related. Some senior lawyers may be such curmudgeons or social misfits that they really do not get along well in larger groups. Others may be emotionally needy or explosive and thus quite difficult for most people to work with and for. In some of the worst cases, senior lawyers may have histories of improper romantic advances toward their aides. Where such problems are apparent, not even the unique benefits of the aide role may justify the risk that the experience will simply be miserable.

Getting In and Getting Out

Unlike the military, where roles are clearly defined, in a law firm senior lawyers rarely state their desire for an aide expressly. Junior lawyers tend to drift into the role, taking on more and more work for the same senior lawyer. At some point, openly or tacitly, there will develop some understanding that all the senior lawyer's work (or work in a particular category or for a particular client) will be done with the aide.

Because the relationship may develop gradually and without an express agreement on its terms and tenure, misunderstandings may develop. The junior lawyer who does not intend to step into the aide role needs to make clear to the senior lawyer (and especially to other senior lawyers and clients) that he/she intends to work on projects other than those supervised by the particular senior lawyer. Such clarification is especially necessary to avoid the possibility that a senior lawyer will presume, erroneously, that he/she has reserved an aide for his/her work, only to be disappointed when the supposed aide does not comply.

At some point, the aide/senior relationship, even where expressly acknowledged, should end. The junior lawyer will have gathered most of the skills and experiences that are possible under the circumstances. The junior lawyer's billing rate and seniority, moreover, may no longer be appropriate to the aide-de-camp role. The question, whenever that point comes, is how best to handle the transition from aide to independent lawyer.

Perhaps the ideal way to end such relationships involves the incumbent aide helping his/her replacement to become the new aide. Such passing of the torch can provide a useful framework for the transition. When the new aide is trained, the former aide's work is done.

As with many things in law firm life, however, such transitions rarely are completed so smoothly. Even if there are some ragged edges in the transition process, it is very important for the aide to make clear his/her plan for the transition. Perhaps the aide will agree to continue with any of the senior lawyer's ongoing projects but to take on no new projects after a certain point. Perhaps the aide will agree to handle projects for the senior lawyer but only on an independent basis rather than as an aide. In many instances, the aide will continue in that role but will take on more and more independent work from other sources.

The goal of such transition plans is to leave the aide/senior relationship with as much good feeling as was present when the relationship was in place. The more direct and candid both senior lawyer and aide are with each other, the more likely it is that the good feeling will remain intact.

Mutual Benefit

Ultimately, in most aide/senior relationships, the most important factors are the personalities of the lawyers involved. It really does not matter whether the aide is from a top law school with impeccable credentials and superior technical skills if the aide is immature, irritating, and wooden. Similarly, it really does not matter whether the senior lawyer is a renowned expert in his/her field; if the senior lawyer is not stable and genuinely interested in the aide's career, the relationship is bound to fail on some important level. The bond of trust, loyalty, and mutual respect is formed on a personal level that transcends the outer trappings of achievement.

Many, many aide/senior relationships succeed, and succeed quite well. Senior lawyers, on their retirements, often receive tributes from former aides, who report that their service as an aide was one of the best experiences in their careers. Former aides, moreover, often find that their former seniors take a continuing interest in their careers, opening doors for them in the profession and providing career counseling long after the aide/senior relationship has ended. When the opportunity to become an aide is presented, it should be considered seriously. The "look before you leap" advice presented here aims to help ensure that such relationships succeed as often as possible.

WHEN THE PARTNER PROCRASTINATES

Virtually every busy lawyer has dealt with emergencies where round-the-clock work must be done to meet critical deadlines. But what if the emergency is not the product of the project but is caused by the procrastination of the supervising partner (or another senior lawyer) who refuses to give you timely directions or a decision on an issue that is basic to your work? This section aims to provide some practical advice for dealing with the persistently procrastinating partner.

It is important to note at the outset that procrastination is not always inappropriate. Often, a decision cannot, or should not, be made immediately, for good reason. A few questions to the partner may reveal those reasons and may permit formulation of a plan to deal with the unique circumstances that required delayed decision-making. Indeed, such a strategy, in which the subject is why and how to deal with the delay, may be a particularly valuable learning experience.

It is also important to note that procrastination is often situational. The partner may have several other important projects in process or may have some personal needs to attend to, which temporarily take higher priority than your project. Again, a few (tactful) questions to the partner or to other colleagues in the firm may reveal the nature of the problem and may lead to the formulation of a specific plan to deal with it. For example, it may be possible for the partner to hand off some of the supervisory responsibility to another partner or to reduce the level of supervision to a point that permits you to obtain adequate (but less frequent) direction and the partner to satisfy his or her competing obligations. This kind of discussion, moreover, will permit you to avoid irritating the partner, who may well be trying his or her best to juggle several high-priority issues at once.

That all said, we come to the main point: how to deal with the partner for whom procrastination is a way of life. This problem, of course, comes in many forms. Some procrastinators are just generally unavailable; when you call or stop by for directions, they are always too busy. Others may communicate with you, but will often fail to say definitively how they want important issues to be addressed or will give conflicting directions at different times. Still others are fond of last-minute revisions to your work such that the directions you were following initially ultimately prove to be unreliable.

The consequences of procrastination are not difficult to identify, but they can be devastating. If you are exercising your professional responsibility, you want your work to be done on time and the greatest opportunity to make sure that you "get it right." Last-minute all-night sessions to complete a project that was delayed due to the partner's procrastination can produce mistakes and will almost certainly produce a tremendous amount of stress and resentment in you. More generally, the inefficiency of procrastination can make you less effective as a lawyer. If your projects are not done well or on time, your reputation may suffer needlessly.

Do not let the resentment and frustration produced by a partner's procrastination cloud your judgment. It is easy to label the procrastinating partner as difficult or some other word that suggests that nothing can be done to affect the situation. Though it may be satisfying in the short term, such labeling ultimately is self-defeating because it means that you may miss the opportunity to analyze the partner's behavior, and your response to it, in a way that could produce productive change.

Trying to avoid the partner's influence (refusing to take assignments, claiming to be too busy) may also be a poor solution. Aside from the risk of annoying the partner, there is a more fundamental point. You cannot escape procrastinators. Even if you succeed in avoiding one egregiously procrastinating partner, there will be others (and clients as well). Thus, it is important to develop skills and strategies for dealing with procrastinators. Here are a few suggestions.

- Spend time getting to know the procrastinator's decision-making habits. What works in getting a decision from this person? Is there a best form for seeking guidance? (Short decision memoranda, checklists, or regular "check in" meetings are sometimes effective.) Is there a best time of day to talk to this person? (Some people are only approachable first thing in the morning, before their hectic day is launched; others like to "clear the plate" of incoming mail and calls before they turn to new matters.) Is the partner a generalist in giving directions or does the partner sweat all the details and insist on reviewing all your work? Conversely, are there forms or times that clearly will not work (which should be avoided)? Are there ways of seeking approval that are particularly likely to inflame this partner? Your personal experiences with the partner may be supplemented with information from your colleagues in the firm who may know the partner's style and who may have valuable suggestions for dealing with his or her procrastinating behavior.

- Look for ways to eliminate the need for approval of relatively minor aspects of your work. If you prioritize your dealings with the procrastinator, your frustration level may decline because there will be fewer occasions in which the partner's failure to respond hinders your work. The partner may also come to appreciate that when you ask for directions, you really do need a decision, not simply the partner's blessing on decisions that are otherwise within your discretion.

- Spend time analyzing the project, breaking it into its component parts and "looking around the corners" for problems that may occur. Do not ask the partner to make decisions on all the component parts of the work at once, and certainly not all at the last minute. At the outset, simply seek consultation on the sequence of work and potential problems that you have identified: "Have I properly identified the steps here?" "Do you see any other potential problems?" "Do you agree that I should start with the first step that I have identified?" This kind of dialogue can get the ball rolling for continuing communication throughout the project. In effect, the partner does not make any single decision. Instead, at each juncture, you remind the partner of the outline of work that you have done so far and the next step(s) you propose to take. This continuous check-in process avoids the need for isolated, momentous decisions and turns the approval process into more of a collaboration.

- If the partner is simply not available, it may be impossible to establish a truly collaborative relationship. Even in that situation, however, it may be possible to use a variation on the collaborative approach: that is, you break the project into its component parts and you tell the partner your general plan for the project and your specific plan for the first step. If, after a decent interval and reasonable notice to the partner, you get no response, you embark on the first step and continue the reporting/request for direction process throughout the project.

- It may be very helpful in this vein to establish a written record of your communications with the partner. E-mail is perfect for this purpose. At each step, you can forward a copy of your previous notes on the project with an update on your most recent efforts and plans. At each step the partner can review what you have done and what you propose. At each step you have gotten at least implicit approval for your proposed actions.
- There are more than a few occasions, however, where implicit approval is simply not sufficient. It may be that you do not have a proposed solution to a problem on the project. It may be that the partner has critical information (from the client, for example) that you must receive in order to proceed. It may also be that the decision to be made is so important that implicit approval is inadequate. In these instances, plan for an escalating series of notices to the partner indicating what the decision involves, when it has to be made, and what the consequences may be if no decision is made.
- The first notice should be provided well before the decision must be made and should set out the essential points involved in the decision (and your recommendation, if any). You should also note that you need to get explicit (rather than implicit) approval or directions. As you approach the deadline, make sure that you investigate whether the partner will be physically available to make the decision in the period leading up to the deadline or that you at least know how to reach the partner if he or she must leave the office. Be persistent and use more than one means of communication (call, e-mail, stop by and tell the partner's secretary if you think that will help).
- Plan for the worst. If you do not get directions or a decision, can your work be delayed for some period beyond the deadline? Can you make a tentative decision, to be confirmed when the partner finally focuses on the issue? Can you do a portion of the work that does not require approval or directions?
- If the very worst happens (you try to get a decision from the partner; you get none, and the decision must be made; you give the decision your best shot, and the partner questions you on why you did what you did), make sure that you can honestly hold up your head and say "I tried as hard as I could to get directions here." Although it is not your job to reform the procrastinating partner, an experience like that can be an occasion for you to articulate how you would prefer to proceed in getting directions on future projects. Such a dialogue may lead to improved communications and better decision-making on such projects.

8

Criticism and Reviews

OVERVIEW

Lawyers are among the most critical people on this earth. They are taught in law school to pick arguments apart, to find weak logic, and to advance their positions zealously. Indeed, many are attracted to the profession precisely because they enjoy such verbal combat.

These aggressive instincts, however, are often quite maladaptive in the context of working with senior lawyers and subordinates in a law firm. The lawyer who routinely displays withering criticism, personal attacks, and lack of empathy can poison working relationships with subordinates, preventing learning, interfering with effective teamwork, and increasing the risk of stress and burnout for all. The lawyer who receives such criticism, moreover, may have no idea how to withstand such criticism. This overview aims to provide some practical suggestions for both giving and getting criticism. All of us, no matter what our station in a law firm, have occasion both to give and to get criticism. All of us can improve our skills in both regards.

At the outset, the purpose of criticism should be clear to both the critic and the recipient. Generally, if the goal is to teach the subordinate, to make it easier for him/her to do the job effectively and correctly, then criticism is appropriate and will probably be well received. Indeed, if possible, that express purpose should be explained to the subordinate at the time the criticism is given. If the goal is somewhere off that mark (to punish the subordinate for a mistake, or worse to publicly humiliate the subordinate in order to teach a lesson to his/her peers), then the criticism will likely have little teaching benefit. There are circumstances where a subordinate has truly made a horrible mistake, and the critic may not be able to hold back an emotional reaction to the mistake. In that event, it may be quite appropriate simply to say that the mistake has upset you, and that there will be a need to discuss how to deal with the problem in the future. That critique session, however, should not start until the emotional reaction has been discharged. If the critique session starts in an atmosphere of retribution, very little learning will take place. The most likely reaction will be defensiveness and resentment from the subordinate.

Time is generally the best cure for an emotional reaction. No matter how strong the initial reaction, in most instances, with a little time it will be possible to have a reasoned discussion of the problem and potential solutions.

On the other hand, it is not a good idea to wait so long that the connection between the critique and the problem becomes obscure. Ordinary feedback and comments on a subordinate's work product generally should be provided as soon as possible. Stale comments on a project long forgotten will not likely produce any learning or behavior change.

Brevity and specificity are also key. Even for the most open, self-aware subordinates, there is a natural tension surrounding the criticism process. Often, if a critique rambles on, the subordinate will really hear only one thing, and then begin to tune out. The one thing heard may be a positive remark ("Overall, I thought you did a good job") or a negative one ("I was disappointed in your performance"). The remainder of the monologue may be shut out, with the subordinate fixating on whether he/she did well or poorly. It is better, then, to pick one specific thing about the subordinate's performance that you know is important, that you know can be improved, and for which you know how to give a coherent explanation of the means to improve.

Specificity of direction on how to improve is particularly important. Vague directions that "you should try to do better next time" will leave subordinates with the disquieting sense that they are doing something wrong, but without any reassurance that if they do something in particular, they will improve. Try to put your finger on exactly what it is that was done wrong or inadequately, why it matters, and how it can be improved. In the same vein, if you wish to commend a subordinate for some superior performance, try to be as specific as possible about that praise. Comments like "You're a really good secretary" certainly do not hurt a working relationship, but a more specific "I really like the way you have been organizing the XYZ files; I hope we can do that with the other files as well" is much more likely to move performance in a preferred direction.

Criticism is best when given directly. There are many lawyers, in many law firms, who simply give up on subordinates who do not please them. The silent message ("You are not performing well enough to work for me") produces virtually no learning. Worse yet, there are some who will say nothing to subordinates directly, but who complain bitterly about them to others. When that gossipy criticism filters back (as it almost always does), it produces a distrust that may prevent the formation of a healthy working relationship. Almost as destructive, the midnight voicemail message or e-mail, containing some stinging criticism, may create an emotional backlash in the recipient. Because the critic is not present to explain the background and purpose of the criticism, to listen to the reaction and answer questions, this indirect criticism may also be ineffective, if not destructive.

Indeed, listening to a subordinate's reaction to criticism may give a supervisor critical information about the problem. It may be that the subordinate did not understand the assignment in the first place, that the assignment was beyond his/her skill level, or that the work was inhibited by other assignments. These kinds of issues may be addressed in the continuation of the project, or in the next go-round of projects. Further, listening to a subordinate's reaction to criticism may make it easier to select an appropriate tone and form for criticism of the subordinate in the future.

Finally, some background of empathy is required for any criticism to be successful. It is appropriate to recognize that the subordinate may have an emotional attachment to an issue. Often, for example, when a subordinate makes an egregious error, he/she expects the worst from a supervisor and will not learn much from criticism unless it is prefaced with some reassurance that the supervisor has confidence that the subordinate can avoid such problems in the future. Similarly, when a subordinate has had a rough outing in trying out a new skill (a first deposition or oral argument, for example), it may be necessary to start any critique session with a very specific point of praise ("I thought you did very well when you . . ."). When subordinates believe that they are stupid or incompetent, no amount of criticism may motivate them to change. When they see that they have some capability and that (with experience and effort) they can improve, then they may be motivated to persevere despite setbacks or failures.

On the receiving end of criticism, perspective is often critical. You must recognize that not all managers (especially lawyers) are good at providing criticism. Although a criticism may come in a seemingly hostile, flippant, or vague form, most senior lawyers are truly motivated by a desire to help their subordinates improve. Thus, even if the message of criticism is garbled, take it for what it is worth: potentially valuable information about how you may improve your performance.

Resist the urge to become defensive in response to criticism. A defensive reaction ("That's so unfair," "This was not my fault," or "You don't really know what you're talking about"), no matter how well grounded, is almost certain to cut off the flow of information from the senior lawyer (both during the particular critique session, and perhaps for the future). If the criticism is so harsh that it truly cannot be borne, it is preferable to say something neutral ("I will have to think about what you are saying"), to say nothing at all, or to ask to resume the critique session at a later time.

Ideally, it should even be possible for a subordinate to feed back criticism to the senior lawyer. This feedback can be as simple as "Thank you for taking the time to give me feedback." A subordinate might even more specifically suggest, "I really would appreciate any comments you have on my cross-examination technique." The point is to recognize and encourage a healthy senior/subordinate relationship in which learning and effective teamwork can take place. Those kinds of relationships, in the end, are critical building blocks for any successful law firm.

YOUR ANNUAL REVIEW

For most junior associates in most law firms, the annual review process consists of a brief session, perhaps 15 to 20 minutes, in which one or more practice group heads offer a brief summary of performance and perhaps a few words of general encouragement. Few junior associates leave such sessions with a clear sense of the key skills and experiences they need to develop, much less a clear plan for acquiring such skills and experiences. Yet, because the annual review may be the one real opportunity for a junior lawyer to perform a candid self-assessment with the assistance of knowledgeable senior lawyers, an annual review can and should be part of an associate's essential career development efforts.

This section aims to provide junior lawyers with some basic insight into the annual review process and to suggest some ways by which junior lawyers can maximize the value of the experience. The methods of annual review at an individual firm, of course, may vary from the descriptions set out here. Your approach to the annual review process will, no doubt, require some adaptation.

Begin with the recognition that by the time an annual review takes place, most of the events on which the review is based may be ancient history. Your work on a project that took place nearly 12 months earlier may bear little relation to your work today. That fact should be a source of some comfort and satisfaction. If, in an annual review, you receive criticism for some rookie error that occurred months earlier, you may feel confident that the error will never be repeated.

That recognition, however, also has a more troublesome side. In many firms, written evaluations are prepared and preserved as part of your permanent record. Thus, even though an early difficult experience may have taught you a lesson that you will never forget, there may be a written record of the negative evaluation (unaccompanied by any explanation of why the evaluation was aberrant or how the problem has been remedied), which may be of concern.

Part of the answer to that concern, of course, is the fact that no single evaluation will be dispositive in a junior lawyer's career. Any junior lawyer's reputation is generally made up of the sum of his or her experiences and evaluations from many senior lawyers. Most senior lawyers, moreover, recognize that early evaluations can be particularly erratic, as new lawyers are only beginning to become acclimated to the norms of the full-time practice of law.

Nevertheless, negative evaluations should not be ignored. If possible, they should always be avoided. Part of the solution is simple good work: trying hard to understand assignments; asking questions to make sure that you are on track with your work; and turning in polished, thorough work on-time and in the form requested. But there is another part to avoiding a negative evaluation: preempting the poor review. There will be times in your dealings with senior lawyers when you will be quite sure that something has gone awry. A senior lawyer may directly say that you have messed something up, or the error may be obvious from the circumstances. In some instances, however, the signs may be more subtle. A senior lawyer may take some of your work away from you or assign some of it to another lawyer. Or, a senior lawyer may simply stop talking to you, apparently having concluded that you are not capable or willing to do his or her work.

Be aware of such signs and of your reaction to them. If you find yourself thinking of a senior lawyer as "difficult," "cranky," "demanding," "aloof," or otherwise at odds with you, then there is probably some kind of relationship problem developing. You need to take some affirmative steps to improve your relationship, both to avoid the possibility of a negative evaluation and to maximize the possibility that your further encounters with this lawyer will be more positive.

In most instances, a direct approach is best. Find a time, as soon as you realize that something has gone awry, to spend at least a few minutes alone with the senior lawyer. It may help to enlist the assistance of the lawyer's secretary, who may know the best times to schedule such meetings.

At the meeting, begin with some positive affirmation ("I really like working with you," "I really like this area of the law," "I really want to learn more about this subject," "I really want to do a good job on this project"—whichever of these or other positive statements may be true.) Next, move to some identification of what you think the problem may be ("I did not understand the assignment," "I did not have time to complete the work," "I struggled with the research"—again, adapting the statements to the situation). Finally, ask for some open-ended advice ("How could I do this better next time?" or "Is there anything I should be doing to improve my skills in this area?").

This approach essentially invites a mini-evaluation. You are giving a senior lawyer the opportunity to say to you, in person, what he or she may be thinking about your performance (and what he or she may be tempted to write on your formal evaluation). But more, you are also giving the senior lawyer the opportunity to vent some of his or her frustration (making it less likely to appear in the evaluation). Indeed, you may be mending a broken relationship. Most senior lawyers will give you a great deal of credit for following a direct approach. If the encounter is approached with a positive, enthusiastic attitude from the junior lawyer (essentially "I just want to learn, improve, and contribute"), most senior lawyers will respond in kind. Even quite harshly negative attitudes may be softened. What might have been a very poor review may turn into praise for being forthright, or at least a recognition that, although you initially struggled with a project, you also expressed enthusiasm and a genuine desire to improve.

Heading off negative reviews, moreover, is far preferable to living in fear and self-deception. Many junior lawyers treat an annual evaluation like a trip to the doctor for an annual physical examination. But they are hardly forthcoming with the information from which diagnosis and treatment can be made. Instead, they assume that if the review is not sharply critical, or if the reviewer gives an "on balance" positive summary, then there are no problems to address. Yet, it is quite possible that some senior lawyers may hold unexpressed critical views of your performance, and it is also quite possible that those performing the annual review may fail to give you a complete picture of what senior lawyers have said about you. You must dig for more.

In addition to pursuing the individual oral reviews mentioned here, you should try to develop some agenda for your annual review. The agenda items should consist of at least two or three questions that you believe may be critical to your individual success at the firm. If you have not asked earlier about a difficult assignment with any particular senior lawyer, you should make sure you hear that person's complete review. In addition, your agenda questions can take a wide variety of forms.

- I am working on a lot of projects with Ms. Smith. Is that the kind of work I should be doing at this stage?
- I have been trying to do more work in another area with Mr. Jones. How can I get involved in some of that work?
- I am interested in developing a particular skill. How can that skill best be developed?

- I have been working on one very large project for the past six months. Is that something I should continue?
- I have the possibility of developing some business from a friend. Is that something that I should pursue?
- I am interested in participating in firm business development activities. How can I get started with that?

Full discussion of these types of questions may not be possible in a single brief annual evaluation. But that should not stop you from asking. The point is that an annual evaluation should not lapse into a monologue. You are entitled to focus the review, at least in part, on what matters most to you. You are also well-advised to show your reviewers that you are actively interested in, and thinking about, your own career development. Enthusiasm for the career development process will mark you as more than a mere functionary passing time with little apparent purpose.

And, if the questions raised in an annual review lead to a continuing dialogue with senior lawyers about your career development, so much the better. The more these senior lawyers recognize your needs and interests, the more they can help you (by directing you, for example, to contacts with clients and other senior lawyers who may bring you expanded status and skill sets). In this way, the annual review may become much less the isolated event that often occurs and much more simply one of many mile markers along the road of successful career development.

CHECKING YOUR OWN PROGRESS

The time frame for entry into partnership in major law firms has stretched to longer and longer periods. Nevertheless, for many associates, there is an assumption that the last year in this cycle, the partnership year, is somehow the magic point at which the potential for partnership can, or should, receive an associate's concentrated attention. This view, that the race to partnership is won in the last lap, is unfounded and potentially counterproductive. The reality is that an associate begins to make (or not make) partner long before the partnership vote is taken. Any efforts to improve the potential for partnership or to overcome obstacles that may adversely affect partnership selection are long-term efforts. There is generally no quick fix in the last year of an associate's career that can make up for lost time. Moreover, the good professional habits that mark an associate as a potential partner must be developed early; bad habits may be very difficult to unlearn later.

This section focuses on the earliest years of an associate's career, suggesting some of the milestones and personal metrics that junior associates should focus on in order to stay on the path to partnership. No single treatment of this issue, of course, can account for all the factors that may affect partnership decisions in a specific law firm. You must be a student of your own cultural milieu, seeking to understand how partnership decisions are made at the firm and how you might be judged when those decisions are made.

Begin with formal structure. Most law firms have formal evaluation systems, which a firm begins to apply soon after an associate starts work. Whether associates are formally graded or scored or are merely given annual evaluations of their strengths and weakness, these evaluations establish a record from which a partnership decision may later be made. Consistently mediocre reviews in the early years of a law firm career may be difficult to overcome later. Strongly negative reviews may be impossible to reverse.

As a junior associate interested in the possibility of making partner some day, it is thus important to earn a reputation for excellence from the outset of your career. When you have positive experiences with senior lawyers, moreover, it may be worthwhile ensuring that some record of that experience exists. Most firms, for example, permit associates to affect the evaluation system by requesting that specific senior lawyers evaluate their work. You should, wherever possible, make sure that your positive contributions are recorded in the form of consistent, strong evaluations.

In the opposite direction, if you have had a negative experience with a senior lawyer, and you suspect that you may receive a negative review as a result, you can and should take affirmative steps to ameliorate the situation. The best response in most instances is to speak directly to the senior lawyer. Even if it is not possible to talk the senior lawyer out of a negative review, you will, in most instances, get some credit for being forthright and professional in your approach. You may, in any event, learn something that could help you to avoid a negative result in the future in dealing with this lawyer and other senior lawyers.

In similar ways, development of the skill set necessary to qualify as the kind of fully functioning lawyer who is eligible for partnership is an ongoing process. It should be part of your regular habits to list (mentally, or even better, in writing) the essential skills and experiences that well-regarded senior lawyers in your firm have acquired and to evaluate yourself against these scales. If you are missing one or more essential skills and experiences, you may ultimately place your partnership prospects in jeopardy. It is not possible, in the last year before partnership, to fill gaps in your development to which you have failed to pay attention in the intervening years.

Failure to acquire essential skills and experiences, moreover, may be a barometer of your relations with senior lawyers in the firm. You must ask yourself, candidly, why it is that you are not getting the opportunity to acquire these essential skills and experiences. It may be that the firm only has room for one or two stars in your class, and that you have not been recognized as such an associate. It may also be that your reputation in your firm, your office, or your group is impaired in ways that may discourage senior lawyers from giving you the advanced work that will permit you to learn and to demonstrate your capability of performing at the highest levels. It might also be that your area of practice does not have a sufficient volume of business to keep junior lawyers active at the higher levels of practice. Any of these conclusions may require action, both to improve your skills and experiences and to ameliorate the causes of any persistent inability to develop such essential skills and experiences.

In addition to personal evaluations and skill assessments, however, you need competent information about the partnership selection process itself, as well as your prospects and any obstacles to partnership. It may be that the formal evaluation process will include discussion on these subjects. Some firms, for example, tell associates whether they are on track to be eligible for partnership. Others, at least, explain something of the partnership selection process. Frequently, however, formal reviews focus more on an individual associate's most recent performance rather than provide much tangible information on the prospects for partnership. Some associates misread this failure to communicate, wrongly assuming that, because the firm has not told them that they will not become partners, the opposite must be true, and partnership is assured.

The better assumption, in most instances, is that the failure to offer a formal discussion of partnership potential during an annual review does not mean anything, one way or the other. Often, reviewers may not have a direct hand in partnership decisions and thus cannot give you a reliable answer. In some instances, moreover, the firm has a more or less formal policy never to tell any associates that they should expect to be made a partner.

If substantial information on partnership prospects cannot be obtained through the formal review process, what else can be done? Some information is immediately available simply by observing and investigating the circumstances of recently elevated junior partners. What do these partners exhibit, in terms of background, areas of practice, client contacts, business development activities, and other factors that may be relevant to partnership selection? Direct discussions with these recently elevated partners may answer many of your questions about the paths to partnership at your firm.

If possible, this kind of information should be supplemented with direct discussions with more senior sources. The head of your group or practice team would be ideal for these purposes. The questions you wish to ask ("What do I need to do to make partner?" and "Am I likely to make partner?"), however, may not be easy to ask of these firm leaders. For that reason, many associates turn to mentors, whom they trust to provide confidential, reliable answers to these kinds of questions.

Enlisting the active support of these senior lawyers may also be of great value in the drive to partnership. Mentors and firm leaders can help raise your profile in the firm by putting you in contact with other senior lawyers and important clients. If they are actively involved in the partnership selection process, moreover, they can help greatly by taking your part in the discussions and by enlisting others to your cause. Where there are questions about your qualifications for partnership, for example, a senior lawyer who is familiar with your background may be of crucial value.

Lack of such a mentor to provide you insight into the partnership selection process and to advocate on your behalf may itself be an important measure of your partnership potential. Ask yourself, in all candor, why have you not made significant contact with at least one senior lawyer that you could call a mentor? Is it because you have given inadequate attention to the issue? Is it because you are not naturally inclined to reach out beyond your peer group? Is it because you are not well enough regarded by senior lawyers in your firm? The answers to these kinds of questions may require concerted action to improve your situation.

You must also plan for the possibility that even your best efforts may not improve your partnership potential in the circumstances of your particular firm. In that case, you must give serious thought to your alternatives (a counsel or permanent associate position at the firm, a move to another firm where the potential for elevation to partnership is greater, or a move to a business, government, or academic position, among many other options). The earlier you consider these options, the better your ability to make a successful transition. Even if you choose to wait out the long process to partnership selection and you are selected for partnership, you will not have misspent your time. Awareness that you have options may make it easier to understand that you are making a choice each day to pursue or not to pursue the partnership option. If your choice is to pursue partnership, you should pursue it wholeheartedly, with a real awareness of the everyday dedication required to achieve that goal.

The key to the continuing assessment of partnership potential, however, is to go beyond the diagnostic phase. Your awareness of the factors that might adversely affect your partnership potential must spark creative thinking about the steps you can take to improve your potential. Because most of these steps (development of new skills, work in new areas, association with a wider array of senior lawyers, for example) involve long-term efforts, you need to develop a system to motivate yourself to stick to these efforts and to monitor your progress toward your goals. Again, these efforts at personal assessment and planning will benefit you even after you become a partner. Once the race to partnership is won, there will be new challenges, which will call upon your ability to establish and implement a plan for continued personal development.

9

Recruiting/Placement

LATERAL MOVES

You have made the decision to move from one law firm to another. You have found what you think is the ideal new firm, and have sought and won the job. What can you do to make sure that your lateral move will be as successful as you hope it will be? This section focuses on some suggestions for how to make a lateral transition.

Reality Check

Begin with a reality check. Law firms are fluid, complex organizations. Often, what is true today will not be true tomorrow. Thus, prepare yourself for the very real possibility that what you thought would be your life at the new firm will actually develop into something quite different. A senior partner or practice team may leave the firm. A major client or matter may also change hands or evolve in some other way. Be diligent in investigating such potential changes before you get to the new firm, but also be flexible in the event that some unexpected changes occur after you make your move. Open displays of disappointment or frustration that the job is not what you expected are unlikely to improve your situation.

Further, prepare for the very real possibility that your new firm will do little to help you adjust to a new culture. Law firms are often quite good at recruitment and technical training, but not so good at integrating lateral associates once they have been hired and given orientation on basic administrative functions (how to use the word-processing system and library, for example). Recognize that you will need to do much of the work of introducing yourself to other lawyers at the firm, learning what they do, and showing them how you can be a useful addition to their practice. In effect, the first few months of service at a new law firm constitute a probationary period during which you should treat all the more senior lawyers in the firm as you would new clients to whom you are pitching for business.

Gather Information

Although from the outside many law firms look alike, in reality each firm has a unique history, political system, and culture. Learn as much as you can about the firm, from as many competent sources as possible. Read the firm's recruiting and marketing brochures, its Website content and the message boards and other commentary on the firm's practice. Pay attention also to the firm's client list and major matters. These factors will have a great deal to do with who has power in the firm and where you should look for work that is of interest to you.

Study also the personal histories and characteristics of firm leaders, especially in your practice area. Where are the connections and alliances among senior lawyers? Which lawyers regularly work together? What do the senior lawyers in your practice area look for in choosing junior lawyers for their matters? The answers to these kinds of questions will help you greatly in searching out and getting good work. Knowing something about your new bosses and compatriots may also help you avoid making an unfavorable first impression on the sometimes quirky, demanding lawyers in a new firm.

First Impressions

Even though you may have met many of the firm's lawyers in the interview process, recognize that the first few months at a new firm will be a series of first impressions. Even lawyers who met you during the recruiting process will probably not know the details of your work and capabilities. You will need to show them just how good you are to make a favorable first impression.

Work on shifting your status from outsider to reliable team player as quickly as possible. Do not clutter your office with boxes of unused materials from your old job. Move in with pictures, plants, and other items that show that you feel at home at your new firm.

Go to social functions of every kind, from firm retreats, to group meetings, to cocktail parties. Do not pass up even mundane events like technical training and recruiting dinners. All these can be good opportunities for some one-on-one discussions with other lawyers. Be ready, when such opportunities present themselves, to explain briefly what you do and what your aspirations are at the new firm. Listen attentively and ask questions that are designed to show your knowledge and enthusiasm and to solicit support and involvement from lawyers who may be able to get and give you appropriate work assignments.

Make a checklist of such contacts and (for the ones that seem particularly valuable) make it a point to loop back in some way. A phone call or an in-office visit can help cement in another lawyer's mind the fact that you exist, that you are pleasant and hard-working, and that you are interested in working with him or her.

If there is a dearth of social functions, create some of your own. Start with junior members of the practice teams on which you are invited to work. Invite them to lunch or for coffee. Getting to know them can help you learn some of the informal rules and relationships of the firm and may be a stepping-stone to dealing with more senior lawyers. Be careful, however, to avoid becoming too closely associated with any one junior lawyer who may be interested in getting you to do his or her more menial work. Other junior lawyers, moreover, may have personal problems, or simply want to complain about conditions at the firm. Although you may wish to be sympathetic, do not join a clique of complainers, who can only harm your prospects at a new firm.

Exceed Expectations

All things being equal, senior lawyers are likely to choose associates with whom they are familiar. To overcome that tendency, you will need to perform beyond normal expectations. Make sure that you are perceived as adding value on every project to which you are assigned.

Pay attention to the little details that can make you instantly valuable, no matter what your prior experience. Be available and in touch at all times. Come back regularly to senior lawyers, for directions from them, and updates from you. Be superorganized, such that senior lawyers can rely on you to organize documents, telephone numbers, and other details that they would prefer to delegate.

At the appropriate time, volunteer for extra service to the firm or your practice group. Many firms involve associates in planning social functions (the summer outing, for example). You may also have the opportunity to help with a presentation to your practice group or to help a senior lawyer prepare an article or speech. The firm may offer pro bono work that can get you involved with senior lawyers at a sophisticated level and help demonstrate your well-rounded abilities. Make sure, however, that these volunteer activities do not distract you from substantial, billable assignments.

Take Stock

The first few months of a new position can require significant effort to learn the details of the operation of the firm, to introduce yourself to other lawyers, and to jump start your work on new projects. After a few months, however, you should have a fairly good base of experience on which to take stock of your situation. It is worth comparing the factors that lead you to the new firm and the realities of what you have found. Often, you may discover hidden treasures (interesting lawyers, clients, and projects) that you did not anticipate when you started.

It may be, however, that despite your best efforts, your progress at the new firm has not been as successful as you have hoped. At this point, having given careful thought and diligent energy to the task, you may need to shift your strategy. Often, discussions with one or more senior lawyers with whom you have become acquainted may help you to become more aware of the hot areas of practice and team leaders who are in a position to give you more good work. It may be necessary to concentrate your internal marketing efforts on these areas and these leaders. You may also need to ratchet down your expectations, taking assignments that are perhaps less interesting, to gain experience and connections that can help you go forward.

Eventually, there comes a point in your experience as a lateral when you are largely attuned to the rhythm of your new firm and its practice. You may start to hear questions from junior lawyers, about the firm and its clients, that tell you that they perceive you as an experienced old hand at the firm. You may also find senior lawyers assigning you more significant responsibilities, well beyond what they are willing to give to someone they do not know and trust. Do not give up on your efforts to learn about, and provide better service to, the law firm and its clients; that learning process can last through an entire career. But do stop to congratulate yourself on making a successful lateral move.

A SECOND CAREER IN LAW

The challenge of entry into the full-time practice of law can be substantial for any lawyer freshly emerging from law school. For new lawyers who have spent substantial time in the work force or raising a family prior to law school, there can be some unique additional challenges and opportunities. This section identifies a few of the issues that second-career lawyers may face and offers some practical suggestions on how to respond to those issues.

Blending In and Busting Out

There is no bright line dividing second-career lawyers from their colleagues. Many new lawyers, for example, take time off between college and law school to work, study, or gain other experiences. The length of that period can be short or quite long.

Law school, indeed, tends to wash away the differences between new lawyers who have spent a great deal of time involved in activities other than law before law school and those who have not. Most employers (especially at large law firms), moreover, think of all their new lawyers as just that: new. They do not much distinguish between those who are new to law and those who are new to law but who have substantial additional nonlegal experience.

That fact can be played in either direction. If you wish to blend in with other new lawyers, and not highlight your additional experience, in many environments you can effectively do so. If you follow the ordinary path of the new lawyer (hard work, lots of learning) you will probably be dealt with in the same manner as are your less experienced compatriots.

On the other hand, it is quite possible to give your law firm a pleasant surprise by highlighting some of your unique talents and experiences in the course of dealing with your colleagues and supervisors at the firm. Even though you may have been introduced, generally, to some of the lawyers at the firm during the recruiting process, you probably will have the opportunity to introduce yourself to many other lawyers at the firm in the course of your work. It is worthwhile thinking, in advance, of how you wish to portray yourself in the course of introduction once you are at the firm.

There may be aspects of your prior experience that are immediately transferable to your expected course of work at the law firm. For example, some new lawyers with a science or technical background deliberately choose to pursue work as a lawyer that relates to that background (such as intellectual property law or government regulatory work in a technical/scientific area). If that is your plan, so be it. You may comfortably tell everyone you meet at the law firm that your background is scientific/technical and that you hope to pursue related work at the law firm. You may expect that many lawyers at the firm will quickly come to think of you in those terms.

But what if that is not your plan? What if, in fact, you have gone into law precisely because you want a change from your prior experience? Certainly a part of the solution will be to pick a law firm that offers work in fields outside of your area of prior experience. In addition, however, you will need to think about how you wish to position yourself at the firm once you arrive and begin work.

In general, your focus should be forward-looking. What aspects of law drew you to the profession as a second career? In many instances, second-career lawyers have a clearer, more realistic concept of what they want out of a legal career than do many new lawyers who go straight from college to law school. Emphasizing those elements in encounters with lawyers you meet at the firm will generally serve you well. Thus, for example, if you had a teaching background, you might explain to someone you meet for the first time at the firm that you enjoy being on your feet speaking before an audience; that you like the challenge of taking a difficult concept and explaining it in simple, understandable terms; and that (as a result of your teaching experience) you went to law school hoping to become a successful litigator.

The point is not that each prior experience (science, teaching, or whatever) necessarily leads to a particular second career in law. The point, rather, is that it is possible to pick elements of your prior experience that have some relationship to what you hope to do in law. And when lawyers at your new firm ask (and sooner or later they will ask, or you can tell them) why you chose the law as a second career, you can set the tone of the discussion on terms most likely to be favorable to where you see yourself going at the firm.

Overcoming Negative Perceptions

Despite the increasing experience of law firms with second-career lawyers, there remains a well of ignorance and misunderstanding in some areas. As a second-career lawyer, you may encounter any number of negative perceptions from lawyers who simply do not have enough experience with second-career lawyers to understand their unique capabilities and potential. These negative perceptions can take many forms, such as

- the view that a second-career lawyer "couldn't hack it" in a prior career.
- the view that a second-career lawyer may lack the vigor of a younger colleague.
- the view that a second-career lawyer will not be able to take directions well from younger supervisors.
- the view that a second-career lawyer who took longer to finish law school (perhaps on a night program) somehow is less qualified than a lawyer who followed the ordinary law school course.

At bottom, all these perceptions are mere prejudices, based on the assumption that someone who is different from the usual new lawyer is somehow inadequate or difficult to work with. Confronting such prejudices can be challenging, but not impossible.

Focus, in all events, on the positive. Yours is a path that has not been as easy, perhaps, as those of some of your colleagues. Indeed, some of the prejudices exhibited against second-career lawyers argue this out.

If you have maintained a career (and perhaps a family) while studying at night to obtain a law degree, you have shown dedication and a willingness to work hard. There should also be little question about your vigor; you may actually have done with less sleep during your law school career than have your fellow new lawyers.

The same goes for questions about your ability to work for younger supervisors. It is quite possible that your prior experience put you into contact with a wide range of supervisors (both older and younger). Your ability to function in a diverse working environment may have been established by that prior experience. At a minimum, your maturity may make it easier for you to adopt an attitude of humility ("I know I don't know everything about the law; I want to learn as much as I can") than it is for younger colleagues who may feel that they need to prove themselves as superstars immediately.

You should be prepared to talk about yourself and your experiences in ways that may help to dispel any negative perceptions and that focus on your potential. Indeed, you should take advantage of the fact that your unusual background may often be a subject of curiosity among the lawyers you meet when you begin work at a firm. Respond to such curiosity (which might potentially reveal some prejudice) with your story, emphasizing what you have to offer the firm and its lawyers.

Trading on Prior Experience

Beyond introducing yourself to the lawyers you meet at the firm and making sure that you take steps to confront the prejudices that some of them may have, there are a number of additional steps you may wish to take that can expand your influence and involvement in the firm, based on some of your prior experiences.

- It is possible that a prior employer or acquaintance may be a useful business contact for your new firm. Bring such potential contacts to the attention of the firm, but do not demand that you have sole (or even principal) responsibility for dealing with the potential contact. As a new lawyer, you will not be qualified to perform in such a role. You can, however, be a useful source of introduction of the firm and its senior lawyers, and such an introduction will often be appreciated. Even if the firm chooses not to pursue the contact (due to conflicts or other constraints), your enterprise will most likely be acknowledged.

- It is possible that your membership in a professional organization may be useful to the firm. The organization, for example, might be interested in a seminar put together with lawyers from your firm, and you might help facilitate such a seminar. The organization's members might also be a source of expertise for litigation and other matters involving the firm. Again, if you let senior lawyers at the firm know that you may be able to help with an introduction to the organization, you should get some recognition for your resourcefulness.

- It is possible that your professional experience may be of assistance to the firm on matters unrelated to your chosen area at the firm. For example, if you spent several years as a business executive in Spain, your Spanish language skills might be of use in explaining a corporate document to a Spanish-speaking client. Even if you are a litigator, you should not hesitate to offer assistance outside your area of practice. Your willingness to pitch in may enhance your reputation and status within the firm.

- On a longer-term basis, there may be aspects of your professional experience that will be of use in helping to manage the firm. Your technical knowledge, for example, might make you an ideal addition to the firm committee working on computer upgrades. Your prior human resources experience, similarly, might make you a good addition to the firm's recruiting committee. Study the firm's structure and offer your services where appropriate.

The point, again, is not that your prior experience necessarily must dictate your course at a law firm. But, if you have useful skills and experience, you should think about whether offering your unique talents to the firm may enhance your reputation and status within the firm. Your ability to control your destiny at a law firm depends in part on how well you can match your interests and abilities to the needs of the firm. Fortunately, as a second-career lawyer, you probably have a great deal of experience in setting goals and formulating plans to meet those goals. For you, the second-career lawyer, a law firm likely represents a challenge and an opportunity much like the others you have already mastered.

PARTICIPATING AS A RECRUITER

Not long after you join a law firm (and sometimes even while you are still in law school), you may be asked to participate in the firm's recruiting efforts. Although you may have just spent the past year or so engaged in recruitment from the position as a candidate for employment, you may not be fully prepared to participate effectively as a junior recruiter for the firm. This section aims to provide you with some insights into the recruitment process from the perspective of a junior recruiter.

Begin with the recognition that the firm may have several, to some extent competing, goals in recruitment. The most basic goal is to attract and hire the most qualified candidates possible. By definition, that goal implies its opposite: to reject candidates who are not well-qualified. What qualifications matter and how they are to be assessed, of course, may be a matter for considerable disagreement. Thus, long term, the firm's general goal will be to establish a recruitment process that is reasonable, transparent, and fair. The recruitment process is not simply a matter of separating good and bad candidates. It involves judgment, and how those judgments are made reflects on the overall image of the firm. Your participation in recruitment thus can contribute to (or detract from) the success of the firm. You should, therefore, take the process seriously.

Keep in mind that the firm may have a great deal of information available on the subject of recruitment. Some firms hold seminars or training sessions for recruiters. Many firms have written guidelines and tips for conducting an interview. Almost all firms provide information on the legal aspects of recruiting (itemizing such things as questions that may be considered inappropriate or discriminatory). These materials should be reviewed before you begin to participate as a recruiter. If you have questions about the firm's recruitment practices, moreover, you should ask them of the recruitment supervisors as soon as they occur to you.

Beyond such general preparation, you should spend time thinking about the questions you are likely to be asked by law students, summer associates, and others with whom you may interact in the recruitment process. Some of these questions may be outside your ken at the outset. (Who are the firm's largest clients? What are the biggest growth areas of practice? What has been the effect of the recent recession on the firm's business?) You do not need to know the precise answer to every substantive question, but generally the more you know about the firm and its business, the more comfortable you will feel in the recruiting process. Often, simply reading the firm's promotional material will provide you with basic information that will respond to most frequent inquiries form candidates. If you get a question in an interview where you do not know the answer, say so and offer to get the answer (often easily done simply by asking the next interviewer the question, as part of the hand-off of the candidate). If the question is important enough that you should know the answer, look it up after the interview (or ask someone about it) and make sure you know the answer for the next interview.

In many instances, however, law students and other employment candidates really do not expect a lot of substantive information from junior recruiters. Instead, their questions are much more personal. (What is it like to work here? What are the other lawyers like? Why did you come here?) You should be fully prepared for these kinds of questions. Often, the specific answers to the questions are much less important than the emotional tone conveyed. Most employment candidates want to work at firms where lawyers seem friendly, upbeat, and enthusiastic. If you cannot convey such a tone (because you are having a hectic day, because you have something else that really needs to be done, or otherwise), you probably should not be involved in recruiting, at least for that day. Tell your recruiting supervisor what the problem is and ask to be excused.

Remember also that most candidates want to work at a firm where at least some of the lawyers share some of their background and interests. Responding to this need also requires some homework. Read the candidate's résumé in advance of the interview, and see how many points you have in common. If these points might not be obvious to the candidate, bring some of them up during your conversation. You may also want to mention some other lawyers in the firm who share some of the candidate's background and interests.

Most employment candidates, moreover, are interested in working at a firm that views each lawyer as an individual rather than as a fungible work unit. Some of the factors that may affect a candidate in this regard involve the firm's training and development programs. You should be prepared to discuss such programs (at least relating how they have affected you). In addition, most candidates are flattered when a recruiter expresses more than a superficial interest in them. Strive, therefore, to avoid domination of the conversation. Listen at least as much as you talk. Be interested just as much as you are interesting.

Pay special attention to the downtimes in the interviewing process (leaving your office to take the candidate to the next interview, waiting to be seated for the recruiting lunch). These are points when the candidate will often see you turning off the preprogrammed interview persona and lapsing into something that is much more aloof. Keep the conversation going at all times. Keep at least a few questions at hand, to be asked of the candidate whenever the discussion flags. The sense you should leave with every candidate is that you would, if time permitted, want to keep on developing a relationship with him or her. That sense of the potential for a positive relationship with many lawyers in a firm is precisely what most employment candidates are seeking. Other factors being equal (size of firm, location, areas of practice, and other objective factors), this intangible sense of the possibility of belonging to a community may tip the scales in the choice of employment for many candidates.

In the end, of course, the firm cannot hire all the lawyers it recruits. Your job in the evaluation process that leads to an employment decision is generally not to assess whether the firm has a specific need for a particular employment candidate, but whether the candidate appears to have all the essential qualifications required for the job. In commenting on a candidate's qualifications (in a written interview note or otherwise), pay special attention to any information you may have developed that does not appear on the résumé. Consider also giving your assessment of the candidate's real interest in the firm. It is sometimes easier for those who have recently gone through the interviewing process to tell which candidates are truly interested in a firm and which are interviewing indiscriminately or who are perhaps merely interview "tourists."

If you are sold on a particular candidate (and the remainder of the recruiting team agrees), then do not let the on-campus or office interview be the end of your recruiting endeavors. Often, a follow-up telephone call after an offer is extended can be a crucial step in successful recruitment. Again, show some real interest in the candidate. (Do you have more questions about the firm? What factors are you weighing? Do you want to speak to anyone else at the firm?) In some instances, informal follow-up meetings (for drinks or dinner, for example) may also be appropriate. These efforts obviously take time and resources. Thus, it is of great benefit to be sure that the employment candidates on whom you bestow such extra attention are well qualified and also reasonably likely to accept an offer if it is extended.

The recruiting process, moreover, does not end once a candidate accepts an offer. Summer associates accepted into the firm are essentially on a multiweek recruiting tour. In addition to doing substantive work, they will meet lawyers in the firm, which will help them to make decisions about where they want to work full-time after school. As a junior associate, your contact with summer associates may be a key aspect of their experience and impressions of the firm. Working with summer associates, socializing with them, getting to know them, and answering their questions about the firm—all such activities are vital in developing the positive impressions and nurturing the bonds that will encourage qualified candidates to return to the firm for permanent employment.

As you leave law school and enter the full-time practice of law, you begin to realize that legal practice is not confined to the research and writing skills you developed in law school. As you take part in the recruiting process at a law firm, you are taking part in the management of the firm. Law firms consist of people whose talent and dedication determine the success or failure of the business. Recruiting talented, dedicated lawyers to work at a firm is a critical function. Even as a very junior lawyer, you can have a real impact on that function.

HOW GOVERNMENT SERVICE CAN HELP
PREPARE YOU FOR PRIVATE PRACTICE

Many law students choose government service or a judicial clerkship as a first position after law school. Assuming that you are interested in private practice after government service or clerkship, this section addresses some of the things you can do to maximize the value of such experiences in preparing for private practice.

Begin with the recognition that most law firms view government service and clerkships as quite valuable. Indeed, most law firms give full credit for years in government service or a clerkship as equivalent to years you might have spent as an associate in the firm. Some firms, moreover, pay bonuses (especially to clerks) for signing on to start a private practice career at one of those firms.

Thus, the question is not really whether government service and clerkships are perceived as valuable; they are. But, there are things about government service and clerkships that can provide particularly valuable skills and experiences that you should (if possible) seek to make part of your clerkship or government service. Here are a few suggestions.

- Look for experiences that cannot be duplicated in private practice. But for service in a prosecutor's office, for example, you
  would almost certainly never see how a grand jury works. But
  for government service, you would probably also not see how
  an agency deliberates, or learn the informal rules that can affect
  how agency staff choose to proceed with administrative rule-
  making or enforcement proceedings. When opportunities present themselves in government service to see the inner workings
  of a system, take those opportunities, even if the work is not
  necessarily glamorous.
- Similarly, one of the principal advantages in a clerkship is the
  opportunity to see how a judge makes decisions. Whenever possible, ask the judge for his or her views on the important factors in
  the case, the quality of the advocacy, and the way that the judge
  makes credibility determinations. Learning to think like a judge
  will almost certainly make you a better advocate if and when you
  are standing before a judge in private practice.
- Spend time thinking, moreover, about the various styles of advocacy and lawyering that you observe. Although it is not possible
  (or desirable) to copy another lawyer's style, it is possible to
  observe what consistently works and what consistently fails in
  appearances before your judge or encounters with your agency.
  Note also the things that really irritate you about some lawyers;

strive to eliminate those irritating habits from your own practice once you make the jump to a private firm.

- As part of your clerkship or government service, try also to gauge your reactions to some of the areas of law that you may encounter in private practice. Although clerkships and government service may not be perfect sources of information for making career choices, they can provide you with much more practical experience with the rhythms and styles of different areas of law than you could get from reading cases in law school. Embrace the diversity that can come in a judge's docket and ask yourself which kinds of cases you like more than others and why. Similarly, in government service, many agencies have rotation programs, which can permit you to perform in various roles. Use these opportunities to find out more about your own responses to various parts of the practice of law. Knowing more about what interests and energizes you may help you to make appropriate, sustainable choices for your career in private practice.

- Take advantage of the fact that many judicial chambers and many agencies provide tremendous opportunities for the exercise of responsibility at a very early stage in your career. Do not shrink from the challenging big case. Mastering such problems will give you confidence to master other challenges throughout your career.

- Participate in any training offered through the clerkship or government service. Gather the manuals and handbooks that are standard for agency or courthouse staff. Tour the facilities. Get to know the staff members, who will often remain after you have left. In short, master not only your own job, but also the details of the operation of the institution with which you are associated.

- At the conclusion of your tenure, make sure to take steps to keep in touch with the people you have met. Often, former clerks and government employees form loose associations of colleagues who maintain contacts throughout their careers. Many judges and agencies, moreover, conduct periodic reunions and other functions where these contacts can be nurtured. These contacts can bring advice, support, and introductions, which can be of great benefit in private practice.

- When you get to a firm, take steps to advertise your clerkship or government experience. For example, when inquiries circulate through the firm (as they often do both formally and informally) about the practices and predilections of an agency, court, or judge that you may know, speak up. Even if you cannot contribute a great deal on the merits of the legal issue, your insight and awareness of the personalities and procedures involved may be of great value. Responding to such inquiries and looking for other ways to share your clerkship or government experiences, moreover, can help to knit you into the fabric of the firm, allowing you to make an immediate, noticeable contribution.

- Continue to study, and dedicate yourself to supporting, the institution with which you have been affiliated. Studying the history of a court, or an agency, and the biographies of the judges and agency leaders, should give you perspective and pride about your participation in the institution. Contribute also, if you can, to efforts to improve the functioning of the institution. The sense of doing good, the sense of personal growth and accomplishment, and the sense of being part of a noble tradition in the law are some of the most important reasons why many new lawyers choose clerkships or government service as part of their entry into the profession.

LIFE IN A LAW FIRM AFTER GOVERNMENT SERVICE

There is a myth, often propagated by law students and junior lawyers, that certain judicial clerkships and government jobs provide a guarantee of future success in a legal career—and, in particular, success in a private law firm. As the previous section suggests, clerkships and government service indeed often offer terrific experience at a point in a career where junior lawyers might not otherwise get such experience. Doing good in public service, moreover, can be very rewarding on a personal level. But it is a mistake to assume that getting the perfect clerkship or perfect government job (whatever you conceive those to be) will guarantee your success in a law firm. Such experiences can generate some unique challenges when a lawyer returns to work in a law firm. Those challenges can be identified and overcome. This section will expose, and attempt to deal with, some of those challenges.

Missing the Basics

The first few years in most law firms constitute a period of tremendous professional growth for most new lawyers. In essence, most junior lawyers serve an apprenticeship, during which they learn the practical aspects of the craft. Many law firms, moreover, offer formal training programs for new lawyers, concentrating on many of the basic skills that are essential to survival in the firm.

Junior lawyers who choose judicial clerkships or government service in their first years of practice may thus miss some very valuable basic training and experience. Worse yet, because most law firms classify their associates by year of graduation from law school rather than by years of experience at the firm, junior associates who come from judicial clerkships or government service may find themselves starting a law firm job without all the practical training required for the job, but with supervising lawyers expecting them to perform at a more senior level.

Indeed, in a curious way, the otherwise highly desirable credential of a clerkship or government service may mark a junior lawyer as someone who should be exceptionally adept. When such junior lawyers stumble in their new law firms, the experience can be quite jarring, especially to the junior lawyer who assumes that the transition to private practice will necessarily be easy.

Discovering the Burdens of Having Clients

One of the great things about a clerkship or government service is that there are essentially no clients. Lawyers in such roles generally do not have to keep track of their time; they often do not need to consult with, and obtain approval from, their clients; they have many fewer occasions of conflict between their personal views and the demands of their clients.

Again, early experiences in a law firm, coming out of a clerkship or government service, can often be quite jarring as a result. Many former criminal prosecutors, for example, feel a distinct letdown moving from a situation where the client (the government) is very often victorious, to a situation where clients are likely to lose at least 50 percent of their cases.

On a more mundane level, lawyers coming out of clerkships and government service into private firms often have few of the habits that are native to lawyers in private practice: recording billable time, consulting on status and strategy with clients, performing conflict checks for new clients and new matters. The list of practical administrative skills required for success in private practice is actually quite lengthy.

Newcomer Status

Although a clerkship or government service generally can help open many doors for employment, after you get a job in a law firm, your résumé does not determine your success. The watchword for success in a law firm is performance, not credentials. Junior lawyers who move laterally from clerkships or government service often find the early, probationary period in a law firm stressful, as they must strive to prove that they are as good as their paper credentials suggest.

What is worse, for some lawyers in private firms (especially those who have never held a judicial clerkship or government job) the credential is actually something of a negative. The clannishness that is native to some lawyers in some law firms is reflected in an attitude that essentially says, "Our way is the best; you are not one of us." As a result, some lawyers in private firms can be skeptical, to the point of hostility, of new lawyers who lateral in from clerkships and government service.

Especially in the associate ranks, moreover, there may be some resentment of those who have skipped some of the grunt work of the early years in a law firm. Again, the lawyer coming out of a clerkship or government service who expects to be warmly embraced by compatriots in the firm may be in for something of a shock. Often, the reaction from the other junior associates, who have had time to form their own cohesiveness, is indifference to the new lawyer. Sometimes the reaction is even more hostile, something like "Hey, buddy, what makes you think you're so great?"

Junior lawyers, moreover, can often be quite protective of their relationships with senior lawyers who know their work and who have come to rely upon them. The power and prestige that come from such relationships (and the perception that such relationships are critical to long-term partnership potential) often mean that such relationships are jealously guarded. A junior lawyer who makes a lateral move from a clerkship or government service may find his or her new law firm compatriots taking subtle steps to keep the lateral in a subservient position. Confronting and cutting through such political games may not be very pleasant.

Some Suggested Solutions

Enough of the challenges; you get the picture. Law firm life after a clerkship or government service is not always nirvana. What, then, are some practical solutions to the challenges of starting a job in a law firm after a clerkship or government service?

First, spend some serious effort investigating any law firm that you are considering for employment. How has the firm dealt with former clerks and government employees in the past? Have such laterals generally been successful? Is there a "critical mass" of such laterals, such that you will not be blazing a trail in this area? Does the firm have any mentorship and training programs that are appropriate for laterals in this situation? Try to get the answers to these kinds of questions before you start at a law firm. Beware, moreover, of any firm that tries to gloss over the answers to these important questions.

Second, adopt an attitude of humility when you start work at a law firm after a clerkship or government service. You may be a hot prospect to a recruiter, but once inside the firm, you will need to work hard to catch up on the practical skills that you might not have acquired and to establish connections to your compatriots and potential mentors in the firm. An attitude of "I know that I do not know everything about the private practice of law, but I am excited about applying and extending my previously acquired skills and experiences" will serve you well.

Finally, be reasonable about your expectations in a new law firm and adopt a long-term outlook. The pressures of a law firm (new duties, new skills, demanding partners and clients, long hours, and the inevitable mistakes that any junior lawyer will experience) can initially knock you for a loop, especially if you expect nothing but perfection from yourself. Give yourself a break. Professional development in a law firm often starts at different levels for different lawyers and proceeds at different rates. Mark you own steady progress, rather than compare yourself to others or to some false ideal status you should immediately achieve.

Hold on to your prior experience in government or a clerkship and recognize that in the long run it will provide you with some unique advantages. That such advantages may not prevent you from experiencing some disruption and difficulty in the transition to private practice should not defeat you. You have mastered greater challenges. This too shall pass.

FROM BIG FIRM TO SMALL FIRM

For many lawyers in big law firms, the idea of practice in a small firm may be quite appealing. Small firms often offer independence, opportunity, and quality of life that cannot be matched in a large firm. Aside from idealized notions that the grass may be greener on the other side, however, many large firm lawyers have really not investigated the details of how to make a successful transition from a big firm to a small firm. This section aims to identify some practical issues that should be considered.

Practice Specialty

Not all practice specialties lend themselves well to small firm practice. If yours is a practice that requires big firm resources and that mostly caters to big firm clients, it may be necessary to shift focus when moving to a small firm setting. A securities lawyer for major public companies, for example, may need to refocus on smaller public deals or place emphasis on private placements and other financing for smaller companies.

This refocusing (if necessary), moreover, should not be a matter of discovery sometime after embarking on a small firm career. Most successful small firms have clearly identified target markets and are focused on specific areas of practice. If your focus does not complement the firm's, even if you are a terrific practitioner (and perhaps even a good business developer), your success may be in jeopardy. Choose a firm based on reasonable, immediate practice possibilities.

Business Potential

Directly related to your practice specialty is the question of your potential for developing business in a small firm. Be realistic. Your prior experience is your best guide here. Do you have clients of your own now? Have you at least handled significant matters on a near-solo basis at your current firm? If not, what steps are you taking, or could you take, to develop business of your own at a small firm? The prospects need not all be immediate, but they should be concrete. Expected referrals from your current law firm, or current clients, certainly count as concrete possibilities, but if there are no guarantees of referrals, be honest with yourself about the prospects.

If there are no realistic possibilities for you to develop business of your own at a small firm, then consider how you will likely find work in the small firm setting. What are the levels and dispositions of the senior lawyers in the small firm? Do you expect them to mentor you and develop your potential? Do they have an expanding business base that could accommodate (eventually) an additional partner? Is your specialty in demand and valued at the prospective small firm? In short, will you be more than a functionary if you move to the small firm? If not, then you should consider looking elsewhere.

Consider also your network of personal and professional contacts. Not just clients or current colleagues (although these are certainly important), but former schoolmates, social, civic, political, and religious community contacts—all these may be drawn upon for business referrals. Your participation in these kinds of networks will be a vital aspect of your existence as a small firm lawyer. If your networks are not well developed or if they do not match well with activities of other lawyers at a new, small firm, your success may be in jeopardy.

Finally, consider your ability to continue to develop new skills and new interests as a lawyer at a small firm. Many small firms do not have the time or resources for in-depth, formal practice skills development. What is your plan to compensate in that area? Are you on a practice committee at a local bar association? Do you regularly teach in your area? Are you a frequent participant in CLE panels? What will you do to keep up with developments in your area of practice and make sure that your skills are at the highest level of the profession? These, again, are not issues to be resolved after embarking on a small firm career. You need a realistic sustainable plan for success in this area.

Independence and Judgment

Small firms are especially good places for self-starters and those who are willing to take full responsibility for virtually all aspects of practice. If you are not well-prepared to operate independently, you may suffer through some serious adjustment difficulties. Ask yourself some appropriate questions. Are you technologically inclined? Contrary to some mythology, many of the best small firm practitioners are quite technologically proficient. Their ability to integrate gadgets (cell phones, laptops, PDAs, and the like) into their practice makes them more efficient and improves their ability to serve clients effectively, even though they may often be outside an office setting.

Are you good with support staff? Contrary to some mythology, many of the best-run small firms have very effective (and often very loyal) support staff (paralegals, secretaries, office administrators, and the like). Effective small firm lawyers generally know how to make use of such talents to extend their impact and lighten their administrative loads. Truly effective small firm lawyers, moreover, view support staff as valued colleagues to be developed and retained wherever possible. An attitude of snobbery can be deadly in this regard.

Finally, can you pay attention to the details of practice? A big firm lawyer may sometimes adopt the view that "all I want to do is practice law." For them, there may appear to be the luxury of practice without many of the burdens of administrative detail. Small firm lawyers, however, practice without a safety net. If they do not pay attention to fundamentals (conflict checks, engagement letters, client fiduciary accounts, etc.), they can get in serious trouble. On a more mundane financial level, failure to pay attention to details (retainers, regularized billing and collection, etc.) can cost the firm money. You must be willing to take responsibility for all such administrative details.

Most small firm clients, moreover, expect a high level of personal attention from their lawyers. To be effective, you must be "hands on." If it is not second nature for you to return client calls promptly, for example, your effectiveness as a small firm lawyer may be in doubt.

Firm Management

For many lawyers in a large firm, the firm's management is a distant "they." Management sets compensation, benefits, and policy from afar, with little input from subordinates. The small firm setting is different in many ways. The form and character of management may have a major impact on the success of a junior lawyer. There are several questions to consider.

Is the firm a permanent solo partnership? In some small firms, one lawyer (or perhaps a small group of lawyers) constitutes the profit-sharing element of the firm. Everyone else is an employee, and there is no plan to change the structure of the firm. Learn that structure and that intention in advance and be prepared to live with the consequences. If there is no current plan to add partners, your chances of later talking the small firm's management into changing its structure are low.

Is the firm a one-person show? Even if there are several partners in a firm, it is quite possible that one partner will dominate the firm, both in terms of setting policy and in terms of generating business. Such a structure may be entirely acceptable (in professional firms, there is often a system of rule by benign dictatorship). Your relationship with the most senior member of the firm will, in that case, be absolutely critical to your success. In addition, there may be significant questions about the future of the firm. What will happen if the most senior person retires? In a well-run small firm, the answers to these kinds of important leadership questions should be addressed. You should ask these kinds of questions before joining a small firm.

What are your relations likely to be with other senior lawyers at the firm? Is there anyone with whom you are an obvious mismatch? Will you, by joining the firm, be threatening any of the senior lawyers? Will you be working principally for only one of them? With a small firm, there is nowhere to hide. If there is a clear potential for some conflicts, you must think seriously about whether another firm might better suit you.

Economics

Small firms often have more creative compensation structures than large firms. In addition to regular salary and benefits, you may get bonuses for firm performance or a share in origination of new business. At plaintiffs' firms, for example, you may also be given extra compensation for successful outcomes, such as a portion of the firm's contingency fee payment.

Understandings regarding compensation systems should be discussed in advance of taking a small firm job. If possible, these understandings should be reduced to writing (to avoid confusion or ill will later). The inability of a firm to provide clear, written guidance regarding compensation, moreover, may be a sign of poor management, deserving of further due diligence.

So, too, promises of partnership eligibility (if any) should be clearly stated. If you are uncertain about when you will be considered for partnership, and by what method you will be considered, ask. Vague promises that the firm will try to do the right thing should not suffice.

Have an eye, moreover, for the business management skills of the senior lawyers. Do they seem to have good control over the firm's costs and cash flow? Are they living beyond their means, growing too quickly, or in the upswing of a boom-and-bust cycle that will soon end? These are all highly relevant questions, and ones that, even as a relatively junior lawyer, you are entitled to have answered. Well-run small firms can survive lean times (without shedding staff). Poorly-run firms often must resort to layoffs (or even fold).

Quality of Life

Most lawyers considering small firms do so on the assumption that a small firm will offer better quality of life (fewer hours, more flexibility, a more congenial working atmosphere, and other intangible factors). But this is not always so. Although few small firms have reputations as true sweat shops, there are certainly some small firms where junior lawyers can expect little more than a paycheck and a stack of files to handle. If, from the outset, it appears that the firm may treat you as a fungible working unit, or the latest in a line of "passing through" associates, some hesitation is in order. No matter your star qualities, you will not change this atmosphere.

Healthy signs are those that indicate that the lawyers in a small firm have chosen their position in part based on their own lifestyle interests. Do the lawyers talk about their outside activities? Do they embrace your expression of interest in quality-of-life issues? To a degree (not to be overemphasized) can you see from their pedigrees (schools, prior positions) that they are well qualified but also obviously making a lifestyle choice? These, again, are matters on which you should be satisfied before you start work at a small firm.

Keep in Touch

Leaving a big firm for a small firm involves some fairly substantial changes and challenges. But it is not the end of the world, and it is not irrevocable. Indeed, for some lawyers, leaving a big firm to practice in a small firm does not mean losing touch with former colleagues at all. Quite the opposite. Keeping in contact with former compatriots and mentors at your old firm can mean referral of business, extension of advice and resources, and the ability to extend your reputation through the network of business contacts at your old firm.

Mobility, moreover, is the essential watchword in today's legal profession. It is not unusual at all today for a lawyer to spend some time in a big firm, then move to a small firm, and later move back to the same (or perhaps another) big firm. There are no permanent barriers. A legal career is bounded by talent and personal vision, not by artificial castes. Your choice of position (big firm or small firm, government, legal academia, in-house, or any of the many other careers that lawyers pursue) should reflect what is best suited to your needs and interests as they develop and change over time.

10

Business Development

OVERVIEW

Many associates respond to the words "business development" with a list of unanswered and troubling questions: Do I need to bring in clients to be considered a good lawyer? If I do not bring in clients, will I make partner? How can I work on business development when I am working so hard on billable projects? What is business development, and how do I get started?

The aim of this section is not to try to answer every question, from every associate, in every law firm. It is possible, however, to set out some guidelines that associates can use to help formulate and execute a plan to become involved in business development. In the beginning, the plan may not be highly specific. But having a plan and revising it as time passes during the early years of a career, will generally serve an associate much better than drift and undirected worry about the business development process.

Good Service Is First

No matter what the personal connection, most clients are basically looking for good service at a fair price. In the early years of a career, developing as much expertise as possible in a chosen field is perhaps the most critical element of business development.

Beyond raw legal talent, however, good service encompasses an array of professional habits that junior lawyers should cultivate. Among these are responsiveness (really listening to and understanding a client's problems), timeliness (paying attention to the client's schedule and time constraints), availability and communication (returning telephone calls promptly and keeping the client updated on developments), and efficiency (avoiding overbilling and ensuring that the amount of work performed is appropriate to the client's needs and expectations).

Developing a reputation for skill and good service (both with clients and within the firm) will serve an associate well throughout a legal career. Such a reputation is an essential building block for business development.

Start with Existing Clients

In a very real sense, business development begins as soon as an associate begins work at a law firm. At most larger firms, senior lawyers have choices among the junior lawyers who may be available to work on their projects. In that sense, senior lawyers should be treated like clients. Providing them good service and adding value to their work will lead them to call back for more work. That is the most basic engine of business development.

As time passes, moreover, an associate can expect to begin working more and more independently with the clients of a firm. If an associate has worked diligently at developing legal skills and professional habits, this kind of direct dealing with clients (or with little senior supervision, other than an occasional check-in) can begin quite early in a career. Even though the clients may not be exclusively the associate's and may not have been brought to the firm by the associate, the associate should mark this kind of independent work as a milestone in the business development process.

Do a Little Every Day

The biggest mistake many junior associates make early in their careers is to allow the rush of daily work to crowd out business development activities. The sense that business development is for later in a career must be resisted so that days of delaying business development work do not turn into weeks, months, and eventually years.

Business development, moreover, is a lifelong habit with a very long-term return on investment. It is not surprising that some of the best rainmakers at larger law firms are older. They have, through years of diligent business development, acquired a solid reputation and an extensive network of personal and professional relationships. One can rarely predict when or how such relationships may lead to business, but it is certain that the earlier such relationships are cultivated, the more likely they are to bear fruit, eventually.

At very minimum, keep track of your friends and acquaintances who might have a hand in your business development. Send the occasional note, make the occasional call, to keep in touch. Mark their career developments, as you do your own. When you can, be a good friend in whatever way you can. When you learn of an opportunity to socialize, especially in a professional context, invite your acquaintances. Many firms sponsor social events for precisely this purpose.

These friends and acquaintances may well be lawyers in private practice as you are. Although, in some sense, they are competitors, you should think more long term. There are many occasions when people you know will go in house: at a business or leave law to become a full-time businessperson. Lawyers at other law firms, moreover, may have occasion to refer work to you (in situations of conflict, for example). Keeping in touch with your law school classmates and other lawyer acquaintances thus may serve to put you in a position to receive business over time.

Look for Ways to Burnish Your Professional Reputation

Having good skills and even enjoying a good reputation within a firm are not enough. Associates need to look for ways to expand their reputation to the larger legal and business world. One of the simplest ways to do that is to write and speak on subjects that will help demonstrate an associate's expertise. Generally, no single article or speech will bring an immediate bit of business, but these can be occasions to meet new contacts and to broaden one's reputation. Writing and speaking on a subject may also raise your profile and help confirm your reputation for expertise within your own firm.

In a different way, work with organizations outside the law firm (business associations, civic groups, and the like) can lead to productive new contacts. Often, such work will not strictly involve legal skills, but can be a way to meet new people and show them something of an associate's interests and capabilities.

Be Prepared to Talk about Yourself

Business development, in some regards, is salesmanship. What are being sold are your own services and the services of your firm. To begin a sale, the customer (client) must first know that you exist. Once you have a potential client's attention, however, you need to be prepared to talk to a contact about what you do and why you are good at it.

Begin by practicing a one- or two-sentence introduction. Ask yourself, after you shake hands with a potential client or new contact: How should I describe what I do? You will probably have plenty of opportunities to practice this introduction (with other lawyers you meet in your practice and in the many social situations you encounter in daily life).

You must be prepared, however, to go beyond a simple introduction. You need to have a good mastery of your chosen area of expertise and the ability to talk intelligently about the other resources and lawyers in your firm. Most clients will be quite interested in knowing who is there to support your work, especially in areas outside your immediate area of practice.

In many instances, moreover, an inquiry from a prospective client will require you to refer work outside your area of expertise to another lawyer in your firm. You need to know something of the capabilities of the other lawyers in your firm to make such referrals.

Be Prepared to Turn Away Business

Most law firms have some sense of the types of clients that are good for them (size, area of business activity, types of legal problems, and fee expectations, to name a few potentially relevant factors). In many instances, early business development activities will yield inquiries from potential clients who are not right for you or your firm. You must be prepared to reject such opportunities in a professional and productive way.

Most basically, you need to have some idea of what the ideal client would be like. What are the top 10 to 20 clients of your firm, and what kind of work does the firm do for them? What kinds of clients, in what areas of practice, are the senior lawyers in the firm interested in developing? You need a basic sense of the answers to those kinds of questions.

You also need some familiarity with the new-matter-approval process at your firm. Who approves new matters? What conflict-clearing process must be followed? What forms must be completed? Does the firm require engagement letters or retainers? Do you need to have a partner assigned to supervise your work? Most new prospective clients want a quick answer to whether you can take on their work, and you do not want to lose the opportunity by fumbling the administrative process.

You also need to be certain about what you can and cannot do for a prospective client before the work is accepted by the firm. Ethics and conflicts rules vary from jurisdiction to jurisdiction. Most firms, moreover, have very specific policies on how to handle inquiries from prospects before they become actual clients. Familiarity with these rules and policies is essential.

When work must be turned away, you need to have some strategy to leave the prospective client with a good feeling. There may be a next time for the prospective client, and there may be occasion for the prospect to refer business from others. Letting the prospect down easy generally involves making it clear that you would like to work on the matter, but that you cannot do the work (for some good reason). Often, it is possible to suggest other lawyers at other firms who might be able to handle the matter.

Have Fun

The habit of business development, like any other good habit (prudent diet, healthy exercise) will usually not be maintained if it seems tedious and unpleasant. You need to make certain that the habit can be comfortably incorporated into your daily professional routine so that it does not become a chore.

In that regard, one mistake that some associates make is to think that one single business development activity will immediately lead to significant business. When joining the right club or giving the big speech brings no immediate reward, the associate can become frustrated and abandon all business development activity.

It is often better to view business development as a game, like roulette. The more bets that are on the table, the more likely it is that a turn of the wheel will bring a reward. Mark your progress in business development by how many bets you have on the table, not by whether the wheel has yet turned in your favor.

Individualize Your Plan

An individual associate's business development plan may vary greatly from this general outline. Maybe you have no time for writing and speaking. Maybe you already have one anchor client to whom maximum attention should be paid. Maybe the firm already has a particularized business development strategy that you are being encouraged to support.

No single plan is right for every associate. But having some kind of plan is essential.

Often, the process of creating a plan and sharing it with senior lawyers in the firm may itself bring tremendous rewards. Senior lawyers who see you taking responsibility for participation in the business development process may mark you as someone who is developing well. You may also find that senior lawyers who review your plan may share some of their own business development plans and may be willing to incorporate some of your plans into their own (thus, making you an even more important asset for the firm).

WHAT IN-HOUSE LAWYERS EXPECT
FROM THEIR OUTSIDE COUNSEL

The relationship between in-house lawyers at a corporation or other institution and the outside counsel for the entity can be a matter of some mystery and consternation to junior lawyers at a law firm. For them, often the only world they really know much about is the law firm world. The client's needs and expectations, in many instances, are filtered through partners and other supervising lawyers at the law firm. As a result, for many junior lawyers in a law firm, the clients are really the supervising lawyers at the firm, not the actual clients who pay the firm's bills.

Yet, getting to know the needs and expectations of the firm's clients is generally a matter of great importance for lawyers in a law firm, at least on a long-term basis. It is not possible to give good service to a client without a very good understanding of the client's circumstances. And it is not possible for a junior lawyer to progress substantially without learning enough about client needs to ensure that he or she provides good client service.

This section aims to give a brief summary of some of the concerns that are most likely to animate in-house lawyers at institutional clients in their dealings with outside counsel. The focus is on in-house lawyers because, for most substantial institutional clients, lawyers in the law department or general counsel's office of the institution will be the primary contact between the client and the law firm.

Differences between In-House Counsel Positions and Law Firm Positions

Many in-house lawyers were once lawyers at law firms. They generally know the habits of outside counsel. The reverse, however, is not always true. In-house counsel must operate in an environment that often differs from the environment of a law firm in many ways.

- In-house counsel often do not have the luxury of time to analyze the intricacies of legal questions. For them, often, a series of questions (legal and business related) may arise during the course of a day. The goal for most in-house lawyers is to answer as many of those questions as possible, as quickly and effectively as possible. Most in-house counsel have substantial legal and business experience and are quite capable of handling many such issues.
- In-house lawyers are commanded by their clients (the business leaders and managers at their institutions) to provide practical solutions. For them, a well-reasoned, thorough, but impractical solution (or one that ignores practical implications) may be as useless as no solution at all.
- In-house lawyers are driven by deadlines and schedules that may be quite foreign to their outside counsel. Periodic meetings of business executives, for example, may produce demands for reports and updates from in-house lawyers. For public companies,

periodic disclosures may be key elements of the working patterns of in-house counsel.

- In-house counsel may be subject to nonlegal concerns and constraints that are not immediately known to outside counsel. A law department may have budgetary limits that affect the amount of resources that can be dedicated to a problem. Further, the business as a whole may be subject to budgetary constraints (or cycles of operation) that affect what work can be done and when.

Sensitivity to these kinds of issues is crucial in relations between outside counsel and their in-house counterparts. Often, awareness of such issues and responsiveness to the patterns of practice such issues impose on in-house lawyers may be nearly as important as an outside counsel's substantive ability and experience.

How to Become a Hero to Your In-House Contact

Most in-house lawyers must operate in a system where triage is crucial. There are some issues that matter a great deal, some that matter less, and some that are trivial (or that at least may be safely ignored for an extended period). Similarly, there are some issues for which the legal answer or practical solution is perfectly obvious and easily achievable. Other issues, however, present greater challenges, both in determining the correct legal answer and the appropriate solution. Some issues, indeed, are so cutting edge that there may be virtually no precedent or authority and no practical experience on which to draw.

For most in-house counsel, routine matters, with relatively obvious legal issues and relatively clear practical solutions, are the matters they are most likely to handle themselves. There are, of course, some situations where in-house counsel must delegate legal work to a law firm, simply because the volume of the work cannot be handled in-house. And there are some situations where in-house legal resources do not exist in a particular area, even though the work is relatively routine in that area. Yet, for most in-house lawyers, the circumstances where need for assistance from outside counsel is at its greatest involve weighty matters in areas where uncertainty is substantial and practical solutions not always obvious.

In such circumstances, in-house lawyers expect their outside counsel to apply substantial resources and experience to provide advice and assistance that can be used immediately to implement an effective solution. The key is rapid, in-depth assessment of the problem by the outside counsel and establishment of an effective team to provide the solution. The speed of response may be directly affected by the outside counsel's understanding of the problem. If the outside counsel has no

familiarity with the background of the client and the relevant actors in
the client's organization, it may be difficult to give competent, prompt
advice.

Moreover, because institutional clients may often be slow to engage
outside counsel to address problems that they hope can be handled
in-house, the call to outside counsel may combine all the elements of a
crisis (large or small): a great deal at stake, a great deal of uncertainty,
and a great need for immediate response. The highest priority for
in-house counsel will often be to find outside counsel who can respond
effectively to crisis conditions. Outside counsel who demonstrate such
capabilities will generally be called back for further work, even where
no crisis exists. Thus, developing a reputation for "get it done, whatever
it takes" lawyering is critical to outside counsel's success.

These observations suggest some essential principles for the performance of outside counsel. These principles apply to even the most
junior members of a team.

- Recognize the client's priorities and schedule. You are being well
  paid to work hard when needed, to get the job done on time, and
  with the best possible results.
- Know your client's business, industry, and key players. The more
  you know in advance of the in-house counsel's request for assistance, the less your in-house attorney will have to explain, and the
  faster you can focus on the main problem.
- Think best result, not perfect result. Most clients are realistic and do
  not expect perfection. They will want to know the realistic risks and
  possibilities in a situation, not merely your best arguments and
  hoped-for results. Moreover, they need your advice now, not when
  you have completed a treatise on every nuance and precedent affecting the problem. The "you can't see it until it's finished" approach
  does not work, especially in a crisis. Let your in-house contact know
  your progress and your predictions every step of the way.

How to Avoid Becoming a Goat to Your In-House Contact

Although in law, as in sports, "just win, baby" often seems to be the
motto, there are things beyond successful completion of a project that
can greatly affect relations with an in-house lawyer. Again, these are
matters that can affect even the most junior members of an outside
counsel team.

- Do not exceed budgets without approval. Most in-house attorneys
  have at least a general sense of the costs associated with the matters
  for which they engage outside counsel. In some instances, quite

detailed and restrictive budgets are provided to in-house lawyers by outside counsel. These budgets are generally reported to superiors within the client institution. Major variances from the budget will have adverse consequences for the in-house lawyer and will not be well received. If a new item of work or new member of the outside counsel team must be added, the client should know in advance. Similarly, if a major expense will be incurred (for an expert or service vendor, for example), the client must be consulted in advance.

- Do not generate publicity without approval. Many clients abhor any publicity about legal matters, and virtually every client hates to learn of any adverse publicity generated by something their lawyers have said. Any statements to the press about any matter affecting a client should generally be cleared in advance through your in-house counsel.

- Keep your promises. If you tell your in-house attorney you will do something, make sure you do it. Drafts of documents should be circulated as promised. Telephone calls to adversaries should be made as promised. Research should be performed as promised. The list goes on and on. If you know in advance that you cannot accomplish some work, say so. And if it becomes apparent during the course of work that some task cannot be accomplished, let your in-house contact know as soon as the problem arises.

- Do not overpromise. Do not set yourself up for failure by over-promising results in a matter. Your job is to evaluate risks and possibilities, not to ignore them. Your failure to tell your in-house contact about potential adverse results may hurt you greatly when such results are obtained. Even if all goes well, your in-house contact will appreciate your ability to outline low-, medium-, and high-risk scenarios and consider appropriate responses for each.

- Strive to be efficient. In meetings and phone calls and memoranda to the client, be brief and to the point. Do not do work that the client could do or has already done. Delegate appropriately to your own support staff and junior lawyers.

- Do not disappear. Most in-house counsel expect their outside lawyers to be highly responsive to their needs (and many actually demand that outside counsel be available on a near 24-hour-a-day basis). At a minimum, in-house lawyers expect their calls to be answered promptly and their questions addressed as quickly as possible. If you expect to be unavailable for an extended period (especially when a client's matter is active), you should make sure that the client knows how to reach you (or at least knows who will be in charge of the matter during your absence).

In-House Attorney Pet Peeves

Despite your attempts to provide good service, there may be pet peeves for some in-house lawyers that can overshadow your good work. Some attorneys, for example, are sticklers about their names: Full name and proper spelling on all correspondence are critical. Others may be set off when they see particular kinds of work on a bill; they simply do not believe that a law firm should charge for certain kinds of work.

Your goal, of course, is to provide excellent service at all times. Part of providing excellent service, however, is being aware of, and responsive to, your in-house contact's individual needs and even pet peeves. If you are the junior member of a team, you should ask the more senior members of the team about your in-house contact's likes and dislikes. You should also run copies of all correspondence with your in-house contacts by senior members of the team to make sure your style is acceptable. As you come to have greater experience with an in-house lawyer, moreover, it will be part of your job to inform the other members of your team on any unique demands or developments affecting relations with your in-house contact. In the end, the more everyone knows about the needs and expectations of the client (and the primary contact at the client, the in-house attorney) the greater the likelihood of success for the team (and the firm) as a whole.

VISIBILITY WITHIN THE FIRM

The social environment of a law firm, for many new lawyers, is quite unique. A firm may include elements of the schools you attended, the early jobs you had, and perhaps even some parts of your family life. But none of these experiences will fully prepare you for the complex, seemingly mysterious world of a law firm. In this unique environment, it is tempting to seek a simple path. For many new lawyers, the simple path is hard work. Stay in your office and do what you are told for hours on end, junior lawyers assume, and all will eventually be well.

But a law firm is not an assembly line. A law firm functions on relationships. Senior lawyers have relationships with clients, which must be cultivated and maintained through frequent contacts and communications. Many senior lawyers place the development of client relationships on par with their top professional priorities.

For junior lawyers, similarly, the establishment and maintenance of relationships within the firm must also be a top priority. If you are brilliant, hardworking, conscientious, and capable of developing into an excellent full-fledged lawyer, but you are invisible to most of the firm, your long-term success may be in jeopardy. This section aims to identify a few basic keys to ensure that you develop visibility within your firm.

Begin with your own class of associates. If you were law school classmates or members of the same summer associate class, you may already know some of them. Build on any relationships you already have, or if you know no one, begin to get to know as many of your peers as you can. Your goals may be modest: Everyone in your class should at least know your name, something of your background, and your area(s) of interest at the firm. You should know the same about everyone else at your level. If you had a question about firm policies or senior lawyers, for example, you should feel comfortable discussing such issues with anyone in your class, and they with you.

If you had a more substantive question (about the law in an area, about getting help on a project, or about a particular client), you should have some idea whether one of your classmates could help you. Often, of course, because you are all new lawyers, your classmates may not be able to help. Herein lies the seed of the need to get to know more senior lawyers. It is not, however, simply a matter of improving your ability to draw on the advice and assistance of more senior lawyers. In large part, during the early years of practice, these more senior lawyers are your clients (and potential clients). Development of positive relationships with these lawyers should be among your top professional priorities.

Get to know the supervisors in your practice group. Be aware of their needs. Often, for them, a key element in any positive relationship with a junior lawyer is the willingness and ability of the junior lawyer to pitch in on projects, often at crisis times and at the last minute. Developing a reputation, as a reliable, competent, "can do" team player will generally stand you in very good stead with these supervisors. Development of the opposite reputation—as someone who consistently turns down work, who whines about the quality of work, or who invents excuses whenever problems arise on a project—will have the opposite effect.

Beyond developing a generally positive reputation with your group supervisors, your goal should be to start getting referrals for work from many senior lawyers in your group. Often, such referrals can be quite casual. One senior lawyer may say to another, "Do you know of a good junior person who can handle this project?" You will never know when such conversations take place, and you will thus not have the ability to influence such conversations directly. But that does not mean that you cannot indirectly influence what others think of you and what they say to others about you.

Keep in mind that every project, no matter how dull or tedious it seems to you, is important to the lawyer who assigned it to you.

Approach each assignment with the internal question: "Would you be willing to stake your professional reputation on an assessment of how well you performed on this project?" For the lawyers who supervise you on individual projects, that is almost always the way they think of you. Good service on a particular project plants a seed within the supervising lawyer's mind. The next time an appropriate project arises for you (often, more sophisticated and interesting than the first project), he or she is likely to call you again for further work. And when questions of staffing come up from other senior lawyers, the lawyer who has had experiences with you on prior projects is likely to recommend you.

Beyond good work for your immediate supervisors, you should take steps to ensure that those above you in the hierarchy of your project teams and practice group have some idea of your capabilities and interests. One of the simplest ways to ensure that you get exposure to more senior lawyers is to ask to participate in the team meetings and conference calls that often occur on large projects. Generally, just being recognized as on the team (implicit in the fact that you are at the meeting or on the conference call) may give a boost to your reputation within the group. Often, moreover, there may be an occasion for review of the status of work on segments of the team's overall project. In that instance, you may be recognized as having responsibility for one or more tasks and may even get the chance to describe your work. You need not toot your horn too loudly in such a setting. The point is that the team is putting its trust in you because you are performing well. That implicit point will have an effect on other lawyers no matter precisely what you say. At a minimum, participation in such meetings and conference calls will help you to understand your work better, will often help you to learn the important terms and the identity of players involved in the project, and will generally give you increased confidence that you are becoming integrated into the professional activities of the firm as more than a mere functionary.

Visibility, however, is not pure work. Consider also the many social activities that may be available at the firm. These activities can provide you with additional opportunities to meet other lawyers in the firm, to get to know more about them, and to let them get to know about you and your interests and abilities. The specific form of the activity does not matter. It can be purely social (cocktail receptions and entertainment events, for example), athletic (many firms have teams participating in leagues, and some have occasional athletic outings), educational (continuing legal education and other training events), or administrative (work on a committee or project).

Remember that in any of these social settings your principal goal is to express interest and enthusiasm rather than to make a hard sell of yourself. People respond to others who are interested in them, much more than they respond to others who prattle on about themselves. Ask questions of senior lawyers that will allow them to talk first ("What are you working on these days?" "With whom do you mostly work?" "What do you like most about your work?"). Once you know something about senior lawyers and have shown that you are interested in them, you may have occasion to talk about yourself and perhaps match up some of your own interests and experience with theirs. You may even be able to softly pitch them for the possibility of doing some work for them. Even if your conversations are brief, however, you will have learned something about the senior lawyers and will probably have left them with a positive impression of you. Over time, a series of these kind of encounters will raise your visibility in the firm.

A special note is in order about extremely large law firms (and especially large offices in a law firm). It is tempting in this setting to shut down your socializing instincts. When there are so many lawyers that you cannot imagine getting to know them all, you may just give up on the effort. As a result, your social network may be shrunk to the lawyers on your practice teams and the neighbors on your hall. You may even retreat to your office, closing the door, and simply working until it is time to go home.

Resist the temptation to give up on meeting people in the firm. Even if the task of getting to know everyone is impossible, there is merit in the effort. And there is particular value in getting to know lawyers outside your immediate practice group and teams. If you have questions on substantive law outside your area of expertise, you will do well to have contacts in other areas to whom you can informally address your questions. And there will be many occasions when a lawyer outside your group may have a question or even a large-scale assignment in your area. By making contacts throughout the office and throughout the firm, you will maximize your ability to draw on the resources and client base of the firm. In short, the more people you know, and the more who know you, the better off you will be.

PARTICIPATING IN CONTINUED TRAINING AND DEVELOPMENT

A law firm is the ultimate "elevator resource" business. The essential asset base of any law firm—its lawyers and staff—rides up and down the elevators every day. If they are not well trained and well suited to the services they provide, and if they are not retained at the firm, over time the firm's success will be jeopardized. Yet, there is a widespread attitude among lawyers at many firms that training and development functions are "not part of my job description." This chapter explores some of the rationalizations that can produce resistance to participation in effective training and development, explains a few of the reasons why it is important for lawyers at all levels to participate in the training and development process, and suggests some simple ways by which even the busiest lawyers (even relatively junior lawyers) can participate in that process.

Private Property and the Commons

If you own your own home, you are likely to spend time keeping it well maintained. You cut the grass in the backyard; you paint the house; you rake the leaves. The town commons, however, is not something you own. Thus, although you may care in a general way whether it is well maintained, you probably would not be willing to cut the grass, paint the buildings and rake the leaves on the commons. That, you figure, is someone else's job.

That scenario, of course, is not precisely the same as the circumstance of a law firm, but it is close. The human resources of a law firm are not owned by anyone in particular. They are common resources. Thus, there is a danger that the cultivation and maintenance of these resources may be neglected. Individual justifications for this view may come in many forms.

- Many junior lawyers may view training as exclusively a responsibility of the partners. Indeed, there may appear to be some hubris inherent in one associate claiming that he or she knows so much about a subject that he or she is entitled to teach the subject to others. And yet, for virtually every skill or subject, there is a continuum of experience and ability. Even relatively junior associates may be able to show newcomers many useful techniques for improving practices. At very least, relatively junior lawyers can identify (and help newcomers avoid) some of the common mistakes that they have already made.
- Senior lawyers may adopt the defeatist view that because many junior lawyers may leave a firm in the first few years of practice, there seems to be little point in spending time on training and development. That view ignores the significant morale and quality-control problems that may be created by ignoring training and development. Long term, moreover, that view may seriously jeopardize a firm's recruiting and retention capabilities.
- Some senior lawyers react to the problem by citing billable hours and client cost concerns. Training and development take time, much of which cannot be accounted for with conventional billing. In the short term, therefore, training and development may require some sacrifice (either in billing some time to an office function

rather than a client or in spending time to develop methods that incorporate training and development into client service). In the longer term, however, training and development are critical to a law firm's success.

Importance of Training and Development

No matter your level in a law firm, it is vital to have support for your work. Even the most junior lawyer must be able to rely on secretaries, paralegals, and administrative staff to perform tasks that permit efficient operations. As you move up in the hierarchy of the firm, moreover, this need only increases. In essence, to free a midlevel or senior lawyer for more demanding work, junior lawyers and staff must be well trained and oriented to perform their level of work reliably and efficiently.

Indeed, clients increasingly expect their outside counsel to be able to create a multilevel practice team with the ability to perform well at all levels. Clients also expect that such teams will be well managed and coordinated, such that clients need not always call the most senior (most expensive, and often least available) lawyer to answer their questions and respond to their problems. The inability to establish and manage such teams can become a real detriment to effective client service.

At the law firm itself, moreover, the most senior lawyers in a firm expect their up-and-coming junior lawyers to learn how to delegate to, and manage, subordinates. One of the skills that may differentiate between those who are selected for senior positions (including partnership) and those who are not is the ability to participate in the training and development of junior talent.

Participation in training and development can also add greatly to your efforts to establish yourself as an expert practitioner in your area. The effort to organize and crystallize your thinking on a subject, in order to teach it, often is quite useful. Concepts that may be rattling around in your mind as vague guides may become much clearer when you are forced to articulate them in public. The recognition that comes from becoming a visible teacher (and thus, implicitly, an expert) on a subject may also benefit your status within the firm and within the profession. Indeed, internal training sessions often can easily be converted into articles, speeches, and client seminars, which may become useful business development tools.

How to Participate in Training and Development

Training and development efforts, like any other behavior, must begin with some personal assessment and formulation of a plan that is appropriate to your individual needs and circumstances. Not every lawyer will participate in training and development to the fullest possible extent. What is right for one lawyer may not be right for another. Nevertheless, a resolve to try to do something in the training and development area, and the identification of some steps that can be easily implemented in this area, are the most important elements of the effort. If the plan is simple, logical, and sustainable (not viewed as drudgery but as an opportunity), then it will succeed. If, on the other hand, a lawyer holds on to the notions that this is not an important aspect of the practice of law or that somebody else should perform this function, then no plan will work in practice.

Some potential steps in a training and development plan, ranging generally from the easiest to the most challenging, include the following:

- Identify a need. Perhaps one of the most classic problems in the training and development area is the fact that gaps in a firm's training and development programs are often hiding in plain sight. It may be quite obvious to you that there is a problem. Whenever you find yourself thinking something like "Our junior lawyers just don't seem to know enough about ———," your instinct should be to do more than silently fume. Find out who at the firm takes principal responsibility for coordinating training efforts. If there is no one, contact the head of your practice group or office. Let them know that you think there is a need for training in a specific area and why you think this training is important. In many instances, you may be asked whether you would be willing to provide such training. Even if you are not willing to do the training (due to work constraints or otherwise), you should at least be able to identify the specific elements that should be covered by the training, which will help someone else do the job.
- You may know of good training opportunities through a bar association or CLE program; share these with your firm's training coordinators or other firm administrators. The worst that can happen is that they tell you that the training is not necessary or appropriate. In discussing that conclusion, you may learn a great deal about the firm's training and development programs and priorities. At a minimum, you will demonstrate your enthusiasm and willingness to participate in the management of the firm.
- Identify reference materials. In the course of your practice, you may discover useful materials of various types (articles, books, outlines, sample documents, and other items). If you find something that is particularly useful, share it with others. Consider sending a memo or e-mail to your group or office, referencing the

useful materials. Your office librarians or group administrators may also have a practice of circulating reading materials to lawyers. You may be able to make use of those systems. At a minimum, consider bringing the useful material to the attention of your firm's training coordinators or group heads, who may decide how best to use and distribute the references.

- Identify good teachers. If you have had a very positive learning experience working with a more senior lawyer, encourage him or her to extend the impact of that training by offering an education program to a wider group. Often you may find that such teachers have tutored a number of junior lawyers on an essential aspect of the practice but may simply have never been asked to teach to a larger audience.
- Be a good student model. Set aside the time to attend professional education programs that are meaningful to you; encourage others to do the same. In doing so, you help create an atmosphere where lawyers come to think of training as a normal part of everyday law firm life.
- Take time to correct mistakes. Often, one of the greatest learning opportunities is the occasion when a subordinate makes a mistake. The challenge is to make sure that the mistake does not occur again (on your work or on any other lawyer's projects). Assign yourself the responsibility for raising the issue on the next available occasion. Such a conversation may be a brief, natural part of daily interactions. In some instances, however—as when a project ends or a lawyer is out of town for an extended period—there may be a lapse of time between the time that the mistake appears and when you have time to discuss it. If the mistake was important enough to cause you concern, however, you must put the corrective discussion on your "to do" list.
- Listen to your subordinates. The only way to discover what level of mastery your subordinates have of substantive law and practice skills in your area is to ask them questions and closely observe their performance. Merely issuing commands is not enough. When it becomes apparent that a subordinate requires additional training in a particular area, refer him or her to a resource that you think might be helpful. Such resources could include treatises, articles, or courses on a subject of interest. Such resources, however, may also include experience working on certain types of matters or working with specific lawyers, which can extend their knowledge and skills in the required area. Encourage and facilitate such assignments where possible.
- Become a mentor. Where you see the potential for growth in a subordinate from developing a more continuous relationship with

you, offer to become a mentor. Many firms support such relationships through formal programs. Even if there is no formal program, however, a simple reminder to yourself to check in periodically with your mentee to discuss progress, interests, and any problems can be a vital method of fostering development.

• Teach, teach, teach. Where you know there is a need for training in a particular area, and you also know that you are qualified to teach in that area, offer to teach. Contact your training coordinator or group head to make arrangements. Your commitment to teach need not be burdensome. Often, a training program need only be offered once every few years to be effective. It may be possible after a time or two teaching a subject, moreover, to hand off teaching responsibility to a colleague or subordinate who has developed a similar skill and interest in teaching.

CONCLUSION

The responsibility for training and development in a law firm is part of every lawyer's job. Training and development efforts need not be onerous or particularly time-consuming. Even the smallest efforts, over time, can make a large difference in improving the effectiveness of the firm's lawyers and staff and in enhancing the professional atmosphere of the firm.

11

Partnership and Beyond

MAKING PARTNER

A cute television advertisement showed a young suitor attempting to convince his girlfriend that they should be married, based on bar graphs and pie charts showing such things as his escalating income potential and other objective measures of his desirability as a mate. The advertisement produced laughs because most people do not choose their spouses in that kind of cold calculation of worth. Indeed, the subjective elements of love and affection can bring together two people who, on paper at least, would appear not to be a particularly good match. And we cluck, knowingly, that the marriage will never last when we see someone ignore love and affection to marry for mere convenience or wealth.

Marriage is perhaps not the perfect analogy to partnership in a law firm, but the two institutions share enough characteristics that a comparison is worthwhile. Just as one could not possibly say that a person who makes a lot of money is automatically a desirable spouse, so too an associate who bills some phenomenal number of hours per year (fill in your own preferred large figure here) is not automatically an ideal candidate for partnership.

To be sure, a hardworking associate is generally very well appreciated by the partners in any law firm. Work habits tend to be consistent over time. The hardworking associate of today will likely be equally hardworking if made a partner. Volume of work may also be a useful surrogate measure for some of the more subjective characteristics of superb lawyers. Talented, effective associates are often well recognized as such by senior lawyers, and they tend to be very busy as a result.

Nevertheless, an associate can amass a tremendous number of billable hours and still not acquire the essential skills required to function as an independent, productive partner. Indeed, for some associates, workaholism may betray a lack of balance that may eventually lead to burnout and at very least may be a marker for social ineptitude.

From the associate's perspective, moreover, it is a potentially colossal mistake to assume that "all I really need to do is to put in my time." Most firms will view hard work (within reason) as a necessary, but not sufficient, condition for admission to partnership. Associates must ask themselves what else they can do to enhance their perceived value to the firm and maximize their potential for partnership. Keeping that question firmly in mind often requires some critical self-examination.

- Do you really want to be a partner in your firm? That may sound like a crazy question, given the subject of this chapter, but it is fair to say that enthusiasm and real interest in participating in the affairs of a firm are among the qualities that can determine whether an associate becomes a partner. Given an unstable legal climate, where associates often depart their first law firms after only a few years or pull up stakes for the promised land of dot-com riches, many law firm partners see junior lawyers as transitory players at best and fungible at worst. Beating back that attitude requires a genuine, demonstrated affiliation with the firm. Taking part in the administration of the firm (recruiting, training, practice committees, etc.) can be an important way to show that you view yourself as more than just an employee of the firm.

- Do you like the partners in your firm? These are the people who will be reviewing your partnership candidacy (or at least writing the evaluations that will be received by the partnership committee). If you do not like any of them, it is a fair bet that few of them like you, and your partnership potential will suffer. Further, if you truly find the partners in your firm off-putting or dull, it may be very difficult to demonstrate the kind of people skills that, in the microcosm of the law firm, may indicate your potential for client counseling and business development. Admission to partnership is not a mere popularity contest. Still, some ability to socialize with the firm's partners—and interest in doing so—is generally a presumptive requirement for partners-to-be.

- What is your business development potential? Most associates shudder to think about this question. They have no clients of their own, and the chances that some acquaintance like a college pal will strike it rich and give them legal work is just that—a mere chance. The prospect for an associate getting immediate work as a partner, however, is not generally the determinative factor in partnership decisions. Instead, firms look at an associate's potential to help in the business development process. Associates who are not afraid of client contact, who willingly participate in client pitches and beauty contests, and who show some outside interests (writing, lecturing, participating in business networks and social organizations, etc.) show business development potential even if they have no clients (and no prospect for clients) of their own.

- What are you doing to expand your interests as a lawyer? Many associates are tempted to look for a safe niche at their firms (a big client, a hot practice area, or a unique set of skills). They fantasize that the firm must make them a partner because the firm needs them. In some rare cases, the fantasy may be real. Given rapid changes in the economy and in the legal profession, however, it is a mistake to assume that the hot areas of practice of today will not cool off tomorrow. Thus, associates with high-quality basic skills (research, writing, negotiating, etc.), coupled with a wide-ranging interest in new practice areas and new professional challenges may be seen as having at least as much value as associates with niche position(s) only. Associates in niche positions, moreover, must be ever watchful for changes in the firm's client base and practice orientation and must be prepared to change focus whenever appropriate.

- Are you making progress as an associate? For most practice areas, it is possible to chart a course of progress in the development of skills and experiences that will eventually permit an associate to function as an independent, fully functioning lawyer (partner). In litigation, for example, most associates begin with tasks like research and office memoranda; then drafting pleadings and discovery documents; then helping another lawyer to prepare for and participate in depositions, arguments, and hearings. Eventually, the associates begin to perform these tasks themselves and move on to higher-order work (supervising junior lawyers, client counseling, etc.). The course is rarely straight. On some projects, the work may be closer to the basic end of the scale; on others, more advanced. Over time, however, an associate should be able to judge (on both a quantitative and qualitative basis) whether progress is being made.

- What was your biggest mess-up and what have you done about it? Every associate has at least one horror story to tell about some deal or some case that went terribly wrong and for which the associate (rightly or wrongly) took the blame. You can run from these kinds of problems, but you cannot hide. If the mess-up left a bad taste for the attorneys who supervised you on the project, you need to be sure they know that the mess-up is out of character for you and that you are taking steps to prevent it (or something like it) from happening again. You will need to work doubly hard to ensure that you have the skills and the discipline to prevent the problem from recurring. Protests that the problem was not really your fault (even if true) will rarely suffice to cure your image problem (and may actually make the problem worse).

- Are you stable? Law firms require teamwork to succeed. Associates who are emotionally unstable, irrational, or quick to anger cannot function well in a team and will have particular problems supervising and inspiring others. Those who demonstrate a supportive, flexible attitude toward juniors and staff, who teach rather than merely demand, and who can maintain good humor and esprit de corps, even in tough circumstances, are more likely to get the partnership nod.

This list, of course, is incomplete. There is no perfect law firm partner and no perfect associate candidate. Each has different strengths and weaknesses. Each law firm, moreover, has different needs and interests. What is clear, however, is that law firms are run by and for people. They are not mere factories where the only criterion of excellence is output (billable hours). You cannot bill your way to partnership, and even if you can, you will miss much of the satisfaction of the professional development experience along the route to partnership and beyond.

BEYOND PARTNERSHIP

Entry into the partnership of a law firm is not a magic process. Aside from receiving the news that you have been invited into the partnership, there is no sudden transformation of status or duties. Instead, the process of transition into partnership is often quite gradual. You may feel like a citizen of both countries (associate land and partner land) for quite a long time. Indeed, there is a real danger of letdown after being chosen for partnership. An attitude of "Is that all there is" can set in. Coupled with the stress of new responsibilities and expectations (often self-imposed), the transition can be difficult.

This chapter seeks to outline a few of the most important points to keep in mind in the transition to partnership and beyond. As with all things, your mileage may vary; the circumstances of your firm and your transition to partnership will be unique to you. What matters is your awareness of the issues and problems. Your solutions, however, will be your own.

Broaden Your Horizons

Often, the path to partnership leads an associate to specialize in an area of law, an industry, or even in the affairs of one particular client.

The idea (perfectly valid for purposes of making partner) is to demonstrate mastery of an area and demonstrate usefulness to the firm based on concentration in that area.

But overspecialization can be a trap for a partner. If there is only one thing that you can do well as a partner, there is a danger that your value to the firm will diminish if that area of specialization becomes less important to the firm. Continued overconcentration in a single area, moreover, can burn out even the most resilient partners over the long term. When work becomes dull and rote, it becomes difficult to do the work well. For business development purposes, as well, it will become increasingly important that you have wide knowledge of law, business, and the activities of your firm.

Make sure that you continue your professional education. Do not restrict yourself to mandatory CLE programs or seminars in your area of practice. Reach out for training (and reading) on subjects that are tangential to, but likely to be useful in, your practice.

Make sure to associate with colleagues in your firm who practice in areas other than your own. Your ability to converse with them and to understand their work and capabilities will pay off in similar ability to converse with clients about aspects of law beyond your own practice and to recommend appropriate colleagues to assist on matters that are outside your ken.

Learn to Delegate

One of the work habits that most likely got you to the level of partner is your attention to detail and persistence. You are probably convinced, moreover, that "If you want something done right, you should do it yourself." There may be a small sense in which it occurs to you that giving work to other lawyers is lazy (or even risks revealing that you are not critical to the operation of the firm).

Failure to delegate, however, for most partners is a serious error. You cannot be effective in the higher-order functions of partnership (client consultation, strategic thinking, business development, and similar activities) if you are constantly spending time on minutiae. Nor can you juggle the conflicting schedule demands of partnership if you do not have a trained, reliable corps of junior lawyers who are available to assist you (and often substitute for you). The experience of partnership, moreover, may become miserable if you find yourself working just as hard as before you became a partner but with added pressures to take on new responsibilities in management of the firm and client relationships.

Make sure that you have at least one junior lawyer (preferably more) on whom you can regularly rely. That person (those persons) should have a very good idea of what is going on in the matters on which you work and should be able to take responsibility for significant parts of such matters.

Make sure that you have a regular system for communicating with the lawyers who work on your matters. Whether you prefer team meetings and conference calls, circulation of "to do" lists, or some other system, you should have a plan for how you will dole out assignments and keep track of their completion.

Make sure that the lawyers who work for you get the training they need. If you see that one of your subordinates is struggling with an assignment or consistently seems to avoid certain types of work, you should determine whether the problem is one of inadequate training and orientation. Take time to explain the issues in your own matters (as part of delegation), but also suggest seminars, books, and other educational opportunities that may make it possible for your subordinates to better understand (and perform) their work.

Accept New Responsibilities

There is a temptation, as a junior lawyer, to assume that the affairs of partnership are all glamorous, high-level matters of steering the ship of state. For many junior partners in many law firms, that is hardly the case. There are a number of "grunt" management assignments that may come your way as a junior partner. Often, these are thankless tasks in the sense that it seems that every lawyer in the firm complains (to some degree or another) about management in the area, but no one seems to want to contribute.

As a new partner you might, for example, be put in charge of managing paraprofessionals at the firm. Every lawyer at the firm sooner or later will need paraprofessional help, and they will complain mightily if they do not get help, or if the help seems somehow inadequate. But, if you ask them to help recruit and train paraprofessionals, you may get little or no support.

You could simply ignore the responsibility and hope that someone else (the head paraprofessional, the office manager, or some junior lawyer) will take up the slack. But that way demonstrates lack of leadership and may disqualify you for more important later work. View the problem as an efficiency game—what is the most effective way to bring order to this problem and to enlist the assistance of others to help solve the problem?

In the same way, approach the other administrative responsibilities of partnership with enthusiasm. Help ensure timely billing of clients. Participate in recruiting and regular evaluations of associates. Make appearances at social functions where partners are expected to attend. These things are all part of the job.

Make Progress

For most lawyers, there are a lot of years to a legal career, and there are phases to any career. In each phase, there should be learning and progress. The progress you make from the beginning to the end of your prelaw school experience, for example, is tremendous. What the ordinary person does not know about law, compared to a freshly graduated law student, is generally quite obvious. In the same way, the learning and experience you will gather in the practice of law between graduation from law school and entry into partnership can (and should) be equally significant. Entry into partnership should not halt your progress as a lawyer. You must, however, mark your progress as a partner on a different scale from the scales that apply to experiences as a law student or junior lawyer.

Make sure that your client development and client counseling skills are progressing. Seek out and accept new opportunities to develop business with new clients or to introduce yourself to existing firm clients. Welcome also opportunities on a more general business development plane (public speaking, writing, involvement in community activities, among others).

Make sure that your involvement in firm management is progressing. Becoming a senior partner in a law firm is not simply a matter of getting older. The more you are aware of the big picture issues that affect the firm, the more you are involved with the senior managers of the firm who are making decisions on these issues, and the more you take responsibility for addressing such issues yourself, the more you should count yourself as a senior partner in the firm.

Make sure that your involvement in the profession and in the community at large is progressing. Lawyers are involved in a self-regulating profession. Lawyers also have unique opportunities to shape the business, political, and social environments in which they are involved. Progress as a lawyer throughout a legal career should include progress in having an impact on the world at large.

Bibliography

The following bibliography is a starting point only. It represents (among other things) a few of the articles and other materials I have recommended to associates in the course of my career. These particular materials are by no means magic. You should consider some of the topics addressed, however, and consider whether you need to gather more information on some of these topics.

Your practice will likely bring you into contact with a variety of materials that may be useful in the course of your career. Make one of your priorities the acquisition of such materials. Inquire of your mentors, colleagues, and supervisors regarding any materials they have found particularly useful. Do not ignore non-law sources of advice. Take insight and inspiration from whatever sources become known to you.

Firm Management

Your firm's manual, Website and brochures. Be aware of what your firm says about its practice and policies.

Martindale-Hubbell directory, www.martindale.com. This directory can quickly provide information on the background of the lawyers in your firm.

Practice Administration

Bar associations: Contact your city, county, state, and national bar associations for information on membership, publications, and committee work.

CLE requirements: Get a copy of your state's Continuing Legal Education guidelines.

Pro bono practices: Get a copy of your firm's guidance on pro bono practices.

Billing/Client Relations

Billing and expense guidelines: Get a copy of your firm's official statements (which may be included in the firm's manual).

Theda C. Snyder, *Why Clients Hate to Pay Legal Bills*, Legal Times, September 9, 1998.

Ethics

James M. Altman, *The Secret about Secrets*, N.Y.L.J., July 14, 2000, at 24.
Jeffrey C. Connor, *The Stress Excuse*, N.Y.L.J., Nov. 26, 2002, at 5.
Mark Hansen, *Tender Traps*, A.B.A.J., December 1998, at 56.

Litigation Basics

Bryan A. Garner, *The Winning Brief: 100 Tips for Persuasive Briefing in Trial and Appellate Court* (1999).
Laurie Phillips, *Producing Data in Discovery: The Key Rules of the Road*, N.Y.L.J., March 16, 1998, at S5.
Edwin J. Wesely & Valerie Fitch, *Pretrial Development in Major Corporate Litigation*, N.Y.S.B.A.J., January 1998, at 25.
What Every Lawyer Needs to Know about Litigation, Loss Prev. J., May 1994, at 6.

Business Practice Basics

Kenneth A. Adams, *Legal Usage in Drafting Corporate Agreements* (2001).
Dennis J. Block & Jonathan M. Hoff, *Underwriter Due Diligence in Securities Offerings*, N.Y.L.J., May 27, 1999, at 5.
Steven T. Taylor, *Client Clamor for Lawyers' Business Skills*, 19:5 Of Counsel, March 6, 2000 at 1.
Corporate Clients' Message to Outside Counsel, N.Y.L.J., August 11, 1998, at 5.
Robert B. Dickie, *Financial Statement Analysis and Business Valuation for the Practical Lawyer* (1998).
Todd R. Pajonas & John A. Frates, *Boilerplate Contract Language May Get You in Hot Water*, N.Y.L.J., Aug. 19, 2002, at 56.
Stanley Siegel, *Accounting "Cheat Sheet"*, Corp. Counsel, Oct. 2002.

Legal Writing

Charles R. Calleros, *Legal Method and Writing* (2002).
Robert R. Cummins, *Basics of Legal Document Preparation* (1996).
Martha Faulk & Irving M. Mehler, *The Elements of Legal Writing: A Guide to the Principles of Writing Clear, Concise and Persuasive Legal Documents* (1996).
Bryan A. Garner, *Legal Writing in Plain English: A Text with Exercises* (2001).

Mark Herrmann, *How to Write: A Memorandum from a Curmudgeon*, 24:1 Litigation, Fall 1997, at 3.

Susan McCloskey, *Recognizing Verbal Clutter: Four Steps to Shorter Documents*, N.Y.S.B.A.J., November 1998, at 8.

Teresa J. Reid Rambo & Leanne J. Pflaum, *Legal Writing by Design: A Guide to Great Briefs and Memos* (2001).

Jane N. Richmond, *Legal Writing: Form and Function* (2002).

Richard C. Wydick, *Plain English for Lawyers* (1994).

Efficiency/Time Management

Aaron L. Danzig, *Increase Efficiency by Cleaning up Your Act*, N.Y.L.J., April 27, 1999, at 5.

Eva Wisnik, *Tips for Managing Time*, N.Y.L.J., September 7, 1999, at 516.

Support Staff

Beth W. Herman, *Treating Paralegals as Professionals*, Legal Times, June 7, 1999, at 54.

Linda F. Little, Doug Rymph & Ann Ladd, *Give Legal Secretaries What They Want and Stop the Revolving Door*, Legal Management, September/October 1998, at 57.

Brett S. Martin, *Working with Support Staff*, The Associate, Spring 1998, at 11.

Career Choices

Deborah Arron, *What Can You Do with a Law Degree?: A Lawyer's Guide to Career Alternatives Inside and around the Law* (1997).

Hal Davis, *Teach Me to Solo: The Nuts and Bolts of Law Practice* (2000).

Hindi Greenberg, *The Lawyer's Career Change Handbook: More Than 300 Things You Can Do with a Law Degree* (1998).

Deborah Guyol & Deborah L. Arron, *The Complete Guide to Contract Lawyering: What Every Lawyer and Law Firm Needs to Know about Temporary Legal Services* (1999).

Kimm Alayne Walton, *America's Greatest Places to Work with a Law Degree and How to Make the Most of Any Job, No Matter Where It Is* (1998).

Harry F. Weyher & Charles S. Lyon, *Hanging Out a Shingle: An Insider's Guide to Starting Your Own Law Firm* (2000).

General

Ted Allen, *What Law School Didn't Teach Us*, Legal Times, May 22, 2000.

David Blend, *Up and Away*, JD Jungle, May 2001, at 53.

JeanMarie Campbell, *How Assignments Work*, Legal Times, Sept. 30, 2002.

Jeffrey C. Connor, *Protégé ISO Mentor*, Legal Times, Sept. 30, 2002.

Jenny B. Davis, *What I Like about My Lawyer*, ABAJ, Jan. 2003, at 33.

James C. Freund, *Don't Screw Up*, N.Y.L.J., February 25, 2000, at 24.

James C. Freund, *So You Screwed Up: Now What?*, N.Y.L.J., May 26, 2000, at 24.

Annette Friend, *What Partners Are Made Of*, Legal Times, Mar. 18, 2002.

Jeffrey A. Fuisz & Alison McKinnell, *Dealing with the Difficult Partner*, N.Y.L.J., October 1, 1999, at 24.

Mark Herrmann & Myriam E. Giles, *This Is What I'm Thinking: A Dialogue between Partner and Associate*, 25:1 Litigation, Fall 1998, at 8.

Linda E. Laufer, *Being Nice Isn't Wimpy, It's a Smart Move*, N.Y.L.J., June 3, 2002.

Tamara Loomis, *10 Tips for New Attorneys on Surviving in Practice*, N.Y.L.J., November 26, 1999, at 24.

Suzanne B. O'Neill & Catherine Gerhauser Sparkman, *From Law School to Law Practice* (1998).

Fernando M. Pinguelo, *Guide to the First Year of Practice*, N.Y.L.J., September 7, 1999, at 5.

Kim Alayne Walton, *What Law School Doesn't Teach . . . But You Really Need to Know* (2000).

About the Author

STEVEN C. BENNETT is a litigation partner in the New York City offices of Jones Day, and a member of the firm's training and recruiting committees. A former Assistant United States Attorney for the Southern District of New York, he has taught at Fordham School of Law and the Brooklyn Law School. His column on career development appears regularly in the *New York Law Journal*.

About the Author